ASHLEY COOPER

THE HOLY LINK OF THE GOD HUMAN ANIMAL BOND

CONTENT

To the GHAB™

"The God who speaks through prophets and parables also speaks through paws and hooves, whiskers, and more."

A. Cooper

FOREWORD

Ashley's work reminds me of this simple but profound statement in Psalm 36:6c:

> *"You, O LORD, save humans and animals alike."*

God's steadfast love, faithfulness, and righteousness—named in Psalm 36:5-6—means the LORD, the God of Israel and creator of the cosmos, intends to deliver both humans and animals as part of God's good creation. God's loving faithfulness extends not only to human beings but to animals as well. God is committed to delivering the whole of creation from its bondage to decay and corruption.

"Yes, Virginia, dogs go to heaven, too." They will populate the new heaven and new earth along with redeemed humanity. And, importantly, they populate the present creation as part of the goodness of what God called "very good" in Genesis 1:31.

It was my pleasure to work with Ashley on her Doctor of Ministry project, which is the beginning of this polished product. I am grateful she continued to pursue and hone her work, and it is a joy to read it again in this new form. Her experience with animals, theological and pastoral training, and passion for animals are evident on every page. This is a rich and passionate theological invitation to love God's creation.

As one might gather from reading the table of contents, she emphasizes the "shared" nature of creaturely existence between humanity and animal life. The link between God, humans, and animals is rooted in God's own act of creation, and God's good creation is designated for "shared life" between humanity and the rest of creation, especially its land, sea, and air inhabitants.

Shared life includes connection, land, place, experience, Spirit, story, wounds, distance, and hope. If you wonder what each of these might mean, that is your invitation to read this book, soak in its theological, practical, and existential meaning, and see the creation with a new set of glasses.

Too often, disciples of Jesus have minimized and sidelined our relationship with the creation. Sometimes we have been made to feel guilty for our attachment to the animals who live with us and share our lives. Ashley gives us a lens that overcomes our potential shame and replaces it with joy, connection, and hopeful expectancy.

The life we share with animals deserves celebration. We ought to enjoy God's gifts, including the connection between humans and animals. The relationships are mutual joy, care, and life.

Perhaps, after reading and reflecting on this book, you will welcome, receive, and enjoy the gift of companionship which God designed for his creatures, whether they live on the land, in the sea, or fly in the air. Thank you, Ashley!

Blessed be the name of the LORD!

John Mark Hicks

PREFACE

Mutuality and connection are my goals when writing about humans and animals, rather than emphasizing hierarchy or dominance in the animal kingdom. Are we willing to imagine crossing interspecies boundaries to embrace other animals as friends, companions, or worshipers of God, deepening our understanding of love and solidarity as part of our Creator's plan? Honestly, ignoring the presence and needs of animals may limit our comprehension of the fullness of the Gospel's call.

I hope you approach this book as you would a good friend, with grace and mercy, as I explore overlooked areas of study, including animals, theology, and spiritual formation. I suggest that missional theology, which involves living a life in service to God and others, invites us to see the Holy Spirit as the One who connects our efforts and creation to the ultimate goal of reconciliation with God. Throughout this book, I will highlight ways relationships intersect, creating opportunities to recognize meaningful spiritual experiences.

Through my research, I have learned that many writers before me have struggled with how to connect the words "human" and "animal" without implying superiority or dominance. By recognizing the inherent worth of all living beings, we open ourselves to a more meaningful and inclusive view of the spiritual journey. This perspective encourages us to look beyond human boundaries and see animals as vital members of God's creation.

AUTHOR'S NOTE ON PROCESS AND ETHICS

Throughout the drafting and revision of this book, I have received help from human editors and digital tools for tasks such as reorganizing material, tightening sentences, and checking for clarity and consistency. All theological claims, interpretations of Scripture, and stories from my life and ministry, however, are my own. Any errors in argument or expression remain my responsibility.

Where personal stories involve identifiable individuals, names and details are used with permission. In cases where consent was not possible or where privacy was a concern, identifying information has been changed.

ACKNOWLEDGMENTS

This book was like a seed planted during the first semester of my Doctor of Ministry Missional Theology course, when we were asked to write a paper, and I chose to write about dogs. From that assignment, the idea began to grow, and I found myself returning to the animals I lived with to ask questions I had not yet asked myself as a vocational chaplain. Including animals in my own theology became necessary because that area had largely gone unexplored until I began to reimagine them as part of spirituality and theological formation.

I am grateful to Dr. Greg McKinzie, whose Missional Theology course created a safe space to make mistakes, to be brave with difficult subjects, and to push beyond perceived limits. His reminder, "This is the place to make mistakes," and his suggestions taught me that it is better to risk errors in the classroom than in ministry without reflection. This philosophy of care gave me the freedom to explore how animals fit within my own theology.

I also wish to thank Drs. John York and John Mark Hicks, my doctoral committee members at Lipscomb's Hazelip School of Theology, with Dr. Hicks serving as chair. Their exceptional guidance throughout my DMin program deepened and widened my spiritual and theological imagination. Through their mentorship, I was encouraged to pursue weighty theological questions and to consider the role of animals within them. Together, Drs. McKinzie, York, and Hicks have served as God's agents of grace, mercy, and wisdom, helping to shape my theological and spiritual ideas.

From there, turning this theological seed into a book required diligent readers and patient editors. Blair Parke was the first to take this manuscript in hand, offering an initial editorial assessment that helped me see what needed reshaping and strengthening. After I reworked that early draft, my primary editor and friend, Falon Barton, DMin, provided more extensive feedback, asking thoughtful questions, making careful line-by-line edits, and offering steady encouragement through the long revisions. After a second major rewrite, Blair returned to the work with a fresh editorial assessment, giving me a clearer sense of where the book had grown and where it still needed refinement. The collaboration between Blair's insights and Falon's detailed, line-by-line work became a kind of shared voice behind this book. Other unseen voices also shared these pages and helped the work evolve into something I could not have created alone.

I thank my spouse of twenty-four years, Jenny Cooper, for the countless times she listened to my questions, reflections, and tangents about this book. She read the manuscript several times and offered encouragement beyond what I could have hoped for, graciously enduring the solitary stretches of writing so this work could come to life.

Finally, I want to thank Winston, Myshka, Twig, Aspen, and Willow for their unconditional love and companionship. Winston offers me such a grounded, loving presence, while Myshka wraps around my legs and is content simply to be with me. A daily dose of Twig's ever-wagging nub was needed on some days to make me smile. Then, there's Aspen, who happily carries my trash to the bin, and Willow, who is known for giving hugs. Their lives have been among my clearest teachers, and their presence has sustained me as I wrote these pages. I also remember with gratitude the animals who have died (Noah, Clover, Psi, Paris, Pearl, Flash, Mo Mo, and Beau), whose lives and losses shaped my understanding as I wrote this book.

INTRODUCTION

The Holy Link of the God–Human–Animal Bond: Reimagining Our Stories to Include Animals helps us rediscover the spiritual importance of our connections with animals. By integrating Christian theology, mysticism, ecological reflection, and storytelling, this book argues that these human–animal relationship, often called the human–animal bond (HAB), are not *just* a relationship but a sacred space where God's presence, love, and mission come together, the God–human–animal bond (the GHAB™). When we overlook God's presence in this bond, we risk missing an important dimension of our theology and practice; when we recognize it, we discover that God's reconciling work in Christ extends not only to human souls but also to the whole community of creation.

In this book, the GHAB describes the living three-way relationship among God, humans, and animals, connected through creation, covenant, and redemption. This bond is seldom abstract and often takes shape in real places like homes, hillsides, barns, and back roads, where our lives and the lives of animals are part of God's ongoing work.

My words and intentions stand in conversation with the ethics involved in animal advocacy work, but they also advance the discussion by highlighting pneumatology, the Holy Spirit as the living "Holy Link" within the GHAB, and pastoral practice, particularly animal-assisted intervention, as a way the *missio Dei* becomes visible in ministry.

Throughout this book, I use the phrase "Holy Link" to describe the Holy Spirit's connective work in the GHAB, the Spirit who continually holds creation together and, at times, makes God's love especially tangible through our relationships with animals, with each moment like a single link in creation's living, breathing, community chain.[1]

Written for pastors, chaplains, spiritual directors, theologians, and animal lovers alike, this book argues that what some call the HAB is, at its core, the GHAB—a living context of God's ongoing mission. Only by recognizing God's presence in this bond can we understand its true nature and missional significance. This recognition is not meant to stay theoretical; it calls us to pray, teach, lead, and live as if God's love flows through the hay fields just as He moves through pulpits and pews. Many readers already feel that their relationships with animals are spiritually meaningful, but they may lack words, categories, or theological permission to describe that significance. Others wonder whether it is appropriate, or even faithful, to speak of God's involvement in such bonds at all. This book is written to address those questions: to reassure readers that their love for animals can be a genuine encounter with God, and to offer practical ways to deepen their prayer, preaching, pastoral care, and daily life.

I write as a practical theologian, but this book is not only for theologians. It is for anyone who has ever loved an animal and wondered what that love has to do with God. My aim is that scholars, pastors, and "regular readers" alike will find language here that helps them recognize and live more faithfully within the GHAB.

At the same time, many of us feel a real tension about when and how to name God's presence in conversations about animals, especially in pluralistic or clinical settings where we want to respect the beliefs of those we serve. Part of the task this book describes is learning to hold that tension faithfully, bearing witness to God's work through animals and places, even when we cannot speak of Him directly.

This book is written to help you notice, honor, and participate in the ways God works through the creatures and places that share your life, and to discern when to explicitly name the Spirit's work and when to let it unfold naturally. Reception history explores how a biblical text has been received, imagined, and used over time in the church's worship, art, preaching, and practice. In this book, I focus on *the history of animal reception*: how animals have been present or imagined in these texts and traditions, and how this shapes our understanding of the GHAB. The book is organized around a series of *shared* themes that demonstrate how the GHAB is discovered within the *missio Dei*.

Below is the chapter's development through a series of "shared" themes that illustrate how the GHAB appears as a real space for God's ongoing mission. The earlier chapters lean more into biblical and theological foundations; the later chapters, especially **"A Shared Wound,"** **"A Shared Distance,"** and **"A Shared Hope,"** knit the themes into our stories and practices so that pastors, chaplains, *and* animal lovers can see how the GHAB is lived in ordinary life.

Chapter 1, "The Missio Dei and the God–Human–Animal Bond: A Practical-Theological Beginning," draws on Arthur Eddington's parable of the fisherman's net to question narrow theological frameworks that overlook animals and creation, inviting readers to refine their "nets" so they can see God's mission to all creation. **"A Shared Connection"** then explores the deep historical and contemporary ties between humans and animals, from domestication and ritual to modern HAB research, therapy work, and the sacredness of the GHAB, showing that these bonds are not accidental but part of how God's presence and care are mediated.

From there, the focus widens to the places where this bond is lived. **"A Shared Land"** portrays the land as an organic web in which God's presence is revealed and shows that living faithfully on shared land is itself a form of participation in the GHAB. **"A Shared Place"** turns to specific locations, both biblical and contemporary, as sites where the Spirit is at work and where creation participates in God's story, often mediating the GHAB as a setting where God's mission with animals and people quietly unfolds. "**A Shared Experience**" reflects on how daily encounters with animals can become mystical "thin places" where the GHAB feels real rather than theoretical, inviting a contemplative attentiveness to God's nearness in ordinary creaturely life.

The middle chapters press more deeply into the life of the Spirit and the stories we share. "**A Shared Spirit**" explicitly turns to pneumatology, presenting the Holy Spirit as the "glue" of the GHAB, the One who breathes life into all creatures and connects every "nowhere" and "everywhere" to divine presence. "**A Shared Story**" invites readers to treat God–human–animal stories as sacred texts in their own right, like *thin places* where the Spirit uses shared experience to form our imaginations, reshape our language, and locate our journeys inside God's larger story of creation, redemption, and new creation.

From that storytelling emerge chapters that reckon with suffering, vocation, and change. "**A Shared Wound**" names the ways humans and animals share trauma, loss, exploitation, ecological harm, and the ordinary ache of finitude, and considers how God meets us there, often through animals' quiet ministry of presence. "**A Shared Distance**" traces how misread dominion, dualism, industrialization, and technology have widened the gap between Western Christians and the rest of creation, then calls us to join God in healing that distance through creation-honoring stewardship, because a Christ-centered life is inseparable from the community of creation. "**A Shared Hope**" stands in that gap and asks what reconciliation could look like in practice. This chapter explores how old scripts of indifference and convenience can be interrupted by the Spirit. We see the hope of creation in Romans 8, which invites readers to reflect on their own stories with animals and places as sites where God's reconciling work is already underway.

NOTES

1. I use "chain" here not to endorse the hierarchical Great Chain of Being but to evoke a lateral, shared web-like pattern of connections in which the Holy Spirit is the source of strength and relation among creatures. For a theological account of creaturely value without axiological hierarchy, see Ryan Darr, "The Great Web of Being: Environmental Ethics without Value Hierarchy," *Religions* 15, no. 5 (2024): 520, *https://doi.org/10.3390/rel15050520* (accessed January 26, 2026).

N. **Methodological Note**: In this book, I'm doing constructive practical theology. I'm not claiming that every biblical text directly teaches a complete doctrine of the GHAB. Rather, taken together with the church's reception history and our lived experiences, Scripture invites us to discern a pattern of God working with, through, and for animals alongside humans.

1

THE MISSIO DEI AND THE GOD–HUMAN–ANIMAL BOND: A PRACTICAL-THEOLOGICAL BEGINNING

After my first donkey, Noah, died, the barn felt painfully empty. His halter still hung on its peg. The feed bucket sat in its usual corner. Morning and evening, the sunset's light fell across an empty stall. The barn had its own kind of silence now, no brays when I opened the door, no rhythmic crunch of hay, no watching me while I cleaned the barn. I kept doing the chores, but they felt more like going through the motions than caring for someone I loved. Grief echoed in the hollow spaces Noah had left behind.

About a year later, I brought home Clover, a miniature donkey I bought from someone who wanted her to go to a good home. Clover had been living with goats and was quite happy helping herself to their food whenever it was served. That worked well for Clover, but not for her health. Like many of us, she needed limits on her "all-you-can-eat" buffet.

When she came home with me, she was not pleased about being on a diet.

We both learned what a grazing muzzle was: a halter for equine animals that limits food intake by covering the mouth while leaving an opening at the bottom so grass can be pulled through. She hated wearing it, and I hated putting it on her. Through Clover, I discovered that a lush green field or acres of tall hay swaying in the wind may look like a gift, but without self-control, it can quickly become dangerous.

Overeating can lead to colic, a painful gastrointestinal problem. Unlike cows, who chew their cud as if pondering life's most profound mysteries, donkeys are more prone to colic from overeating green grass or hay, especially in spring, when the grass is lush and practically begs to be eaten.

Caring for Clover over the years taught me that there are different kinds of colic. Too much sugar from fresh grass can give donkeys a sugar high that inevitably ends in a hard crash. I also learned that mowing the grass, which encourages rapid regrowth, can make it even richer. Eating grass shavings from the mower is essentially a donkey's version of binging on candy bars, an unhealthy indulgence equine veterinarians strongly advise against.

I watched Clover experience episodes of colic-like behavior, like rolling, stomping, and giving me the "please, make it stop" look. Walking her during an episode was like taking a cranky toddler for a stroller ride around the block, but it was just what the doctor ordered. This journey taught me the importance of grazing management, because a donkey can't be healthy if their guardian can't say, "Enough is enough."

Clover did not die of colic, but she taught me a great deal about it because she *loved* food more than anything else.

When I began looking for a companion for Clover, I was given Sandy's number, a connection that would become much deeper than I could have imagined.

About six months after bringing Clover home, my spouse, Jenny, and I went to meet Sandy's herd of miniature donkeys, hoping to find the right match. Among the lively group, one donkey walked right up, sniffing and studying me.

"Who's this?" I asked.

"That's Winston," Sandy replied. "I think he's about four years old. I'd need to look at his registration papers to make sure."

Standing in the middle of Sandy's herd, surrounded by donkeys, we felt both overwhelmed and exhilarated. It was as if the donkeys were welcoming us into their fellowship, a gathering full of food, water, and community, almost like a church social. We couldn't resist the instinct to touch their long, soft ears, until at last, they grew bored with us. As most of the other donkeys wandered away, one donkey came nearer.

"Who is this again?" I asked.

Sandy laughed. "That's Winston. He's coming back for more pets."

I was intrigued. "And he's only four or five? How long do donkeys usually live?"

"They can live to be 30 to 40 years old," she replied.

Jenny, usually a bit shy, broke her silence and shared, "He keeps coming up to you."

I hadn't noticed, distracted by the crowd. "Who, this one?"

"Yeah, that's my youngest one, Winston," Sandy confirmed.

"I want this one," I blurted. Before I'd even consciously thought about it, my spirit and heart knew the connection we had. I placed my hand on Winston as he stepped closer.

Sandy agreed.

Getting Winston into the trailer was an adventure. He was all muscle and refused to leave his herd. With a thick rope and the combined efforts of Jenny, Sandy, and me, we finally coaxed him in, much to the amusement of Sandy's neighbors. Sweaty and exhausted, we shared a collective sigh of relief as we closed the trailer door.

Her patience and guidance over the next several weeks and months helped me see Winston's unique spirit and celebrate our decision to bring him home.

When we arrived, we released Winston into the paddock with Clover. They sniffed each other, stood with their ears back and nostrils flaring, assessing one another. There were no signs of hostility, and I felt hopeful that they would become friends, but I knew only time would tell.

Clover's personality became more apparent to us in contrast with Winston's. She was friendly but aloof. She was no less deserving of care, of course, and we offered her the same attention and tenderness we showed Winston. But she was so much more interested in eating than in socializing, treating Winston and me as little more than a field decoration. I believe she was genuinely unhappy. Restricting her diet was an act of care, but to her, it felt like a loss, perhaps even a cruelty, that she couldn't understand.

If we had not first experienced Clover's apathy toward our attempts to connect, we might not have realized how different Winston was. Her distance only made his affection more noticeable. He showed a surprising inclination to connect with people. His courage to meet new people and his longing for human interaction captivated me, and I became attuned to his gentle spirit.

Curious about Winston's lineage, I pulled out his Miniature Donkey Registry papers and learned of his mother, KAH Clementine, and his father, Lil' Angels Braveheart, a jack known for his rare calmness. That helped explain Winston's own composed and kind nature.

Eventually, I realized Clover might be happier in another home. Her new owner keeps me updated, and I'm grateful to know she's thriving among the other animals.

Winston, on the other hand, has become my companion and friend, a donkey whose presence soothes and comforts not only me but many others. Since 2023, we have been a certified Animal-Assisted Intervention (AAI) team with Pet Partners.[1] In keeping with Pet Partners' standards and my own convictions, I treat Winston not as equipment but as a partner: his participation is always voluntary, and rest and recovery are part of his care. It is from a place of that care that he is able to be present, engaging, and comfort people struggling with mental and physical illnesses. His calm demeanor and his ability to foster peace in those around him have made him a beloved therapy donkey.

From crowded schoolyards to workplace wellness visits, Winston helps foster a *spiritual reset* for many of the people he meets. To me, Winston is more than just a pet and a calming presence; he is a living symbol of God's grace. Our bond is deeply personal, and I can feel God's nearness in the rituals of feeding, grooming, and walking with him. Yet, on nursing home patios and workplace hallways, I see that same bond extend to patients, staff, and strangers who reach out to him. Their breathing slows, their faces change, and something in the room shifts. It is in these recurring moments that I observe the spiritual interconnectedness among God, humans, and animals, a phrase I call the God-human-animal bond, or the GHAB™. The GHAB becomes a lived expression of the Spirit's *kenotic* activity, God's pouring out Himself. The GHAB is a place where God's Spirit works through Winston to calm anxiety, reaffirm hope, and awaken people to the sacredness of their lives and the creatures beside them. God, Jesus, and the Spirit self-empty into us and the world, and then we are empowered by the Spirit as a form of human kenotic participation.

Looking back, these early years with Clover and Winston served as a mini-practicum in practical theology. Through them, God used this time to teach me discernment through the daily grind: learning to read Clover's body language rather than my projections, to treat her discomfort and grazing patterns as a sort of information-gathering rather than mere inconvenience, and to distinguish between what felt comforting to her in the moment and what actually served her long-term well-being. God used this long, messy learning curve as part of His training in caring for Clover. In the same season, God was also shaping my capacity to recognize a bond with Winston, the donkey who kept re-introducing himself, not simply as an overly attached donkey, but as the particular companion whose temperament was a perfect fit for me and, later, for our shared ministry.

THE MISSIO DEI AND THE GHAB

One chilly autumn morning, Winston and I encountered a group of deer at the edge of the woods near our home. Winston probably saw them before I did. Their gaze met ours, and I felt an unexpected connection, a silent acknowledgment that we are part of the same living world. The deer held a long gaze with Winston and me as we slowly walked down the road. Our presence seemed to mesmerize them. Then their hooves began a rustling of leaves, and the sound quickly turned into running and leaping through the field. Just before they ran, there was a moment in time when deer, donkey, and human really saw each other and, in our different ways, recognized that we were sharing this place and this morning together.

I did not yet have the language for it, but that morning with Winston and the deer became part of my missional journey, of learning to see God's presence within creaturely bonds.

They were, I would later realize, moments that exposed the limits of the spiritual "net" we cast over reality, the ways of thinking and seeing that shape how we understand God, mission, and creation.

THROUGH THE LENS OF THE FISHERMAN'S NET

Consider this parable, written by Arthur Eddington, as you think about what your own spiritual nets might be:

Imagine a fisherman exploring the ocean. He casts his net into the water, scoops up a catch, inspects his fish, and shouts, "A-ha! I have made two great scientific discoveries. First, there are no fish smaller than two inches. Second, all fish have gills."[2] Eddington used this image to describe "the structure of thought" and to argue that we cannot know much about the "fish" until we understand the "net," meaning our own ways of thinking and perceiving.

At first glance, these conclusions might seem reasonable. For our purposes, let's focus on the fisherman's first "discovery," which is clearly an error. It is not that there are no fish smaller than two inches, but that his net cannot catch them. The net itself limits the fisherman's observations: the holes are two inches wide, so any fish smaller than that slips through unseen. His second discovery, "all fish have gills," happens to be closer to the truth, but even that truth is shaped by what his net delivers to him. The fisherman is right, but he does not know *why*, nor whether his conclusion would hold if he could see every kind of fish in the sea. Both his mistake and his success arise from the same limitation: he can only describe what his net allows him to see.

Our conceptual nets, like the fisherman's, determine what we are able to notice, measure, and describe. One of Eddington's students, physicist Peter Putnam, expanded on this image in his own work. Scientific author Amanda Gefter mentions in her account of Putnam that he became focused on "a description of the net," a model of "the structure of thought."[3] In other words, while Eddington used the fisherman's net to show the limits of scientific observation, Putnam took the metaphor further, turning it into a project of mapping the net itself. Instead of focusing solely on what the net catches, he was interested in how the net is woven in the first place: the assumptions, categories, and structures of thought that shape every act of knowing.

CONTEXT OF THE GHAB

The fisherman's parable offers a helpful lens for examining the net, which is the set of tools, frameworks, or cognitive structures we use to perceive and interpret reality.

In light of the GHAB, the "net" might symbolize human perception, cultural lenses, or theological constructs through which we understand our relationships within the animal kingdom. Our nets are *finite (*they only catch part of what is really there) and *biased* (they are shaped by our culture, fears, and expectations). God's reality, however, is far richer than what our limited ways of seeing can contain. God is present *in* creation but remains distinct *from* it.

When I first brought Clover home, my "net" was woven mostly from affection and grief, my love for her and my longing to fill the empty space Noah had left. Through that net, I saw a lush pasture as a pure blessing and her constant eating as comfort and contentment, not as a health risk. Only later, through the hard lessons of grazing management and her colic-like episodes, did my net begin to change. The pasture and Clover had not changed; what changed was the kind of net I was using, one that now included veterinary wisdom, boundaries, and a clearer sense of what care required.

Humans naturally view the world through their own perspective, which can lead them to miss important aspects of reality. The fisherman who concludes there are no fish less than two inches illustrates how our assumptions shape what we notice. In faith communities, we often focus on human needs and concerns, unintentionally neglecting the environment around us and its significance in God's broader story. This "net" of human-centered (or even individual-centered) thinking can limit our sense of responsibility and wonder.

As I managed Clover's diet and watched Winston lock eyes with the deer at the tree line, my own "net" initially filtered these events as merely veterinary concerns or charming wildlife encounters. Over time, Scripture and experience further refined that net so that I could also perceive them as intersections of the *missio Dei.*

REFINING OUR NETS FOR INCLUSIVITY

The "fisherman's" parable also helps clarify the scope of God's work in the world. From the beginning, God's covenants have embraced more than humanity (Gen. 9:9–10), and in Christ that same reconciling purpose is said to reach "all things, whether things on earth or things in heaven" (Col. 1:19–20). Read together, these texts suggest a consistent trajectory rather than an isolated proof-text. In Christ, God's reconciling work extends beyond humans; it includes the entire created order, such as a variety of animals, plants, and ecosystems. When we participate in God's reconciling work, it is known as the *missio Dei.* To speak of the *missio Dei*, then, is to confess that God's Triune life is inherently sending and self-giving is *kenotic*, and that doctrine, practice, and spirituality must first be received and embodied at the level of the individual and then, at every level of the church's life, be critically evaluated by the extent to which they participate in and bear witness to this cosmic, cruciform movement of reconciliation. I will elaborate on this phrase in the next section.

In this light, the fisherman's net becomes a way to reflect on how we participate in, or misunderstand, God's work.

The act of casting and hauling in the net illustrates the effort needed to engage with what God is already doing. If we refuse to participate, the "net" stays empty, symbolizing missed chances to gather, nurture, and bear witness.

For example, a community might ignore the fall of ecosystems, missing chances to model God's compassion and stewardship. When churches overlook environmental injustice, they risk neglecting part of what God cares about. Without active, holistic involvement, the potential for healing, growth, and witness diminishes.

If the holes in our theological or spiritual "net" are too large, much of what Colossians 1 and Romans 8 convey can slip through before we have a chance to notice, examine, and understand the fullness of what's there. A narrow focus on human salvation can exclude the redemption of creation, overlooking passages such as Romans 8:19-22, in which the entire creation groans for liberation alongside us. Imagine a church that emphasizes only personal salvation, viewing God's work primarily as saving individual souls for heaven. That facet of salvation is essential, but incomplete. Scripture also speaks of creation itself being set free from bondage.

To stay active in God's work, we must sometimes refine our nets. We may need to deconstruct and reconstruct our theologies, practices, and spiritual disciplines. This involves asking tough questions, embracing humility, and remaining open to the newness God offers.

LIVING INTO THE MISSIO DEI

The mission of God (or *missio Dei*) is a central theme in theology, involving our participation in God's efforts to reconcile all living things to Himself. I will help you reframe the definition in different ways throughout the book. Simply put, it is a broad idea with a meaning that can change depending on the context. Overall, I see the *missio Dei* as more encompassing rather than limited to a single ministry or practice, and mission theology as the study of how we intentionally participate in God's larger mission.

The phrase *missio Dei* originates from Jesus' statement in Jn 20:21: "Peace be with you. As the Father has sent me, even so I am sending you." This underscores that, as followers of Christ, we are called and sent into the world to demonstrate love, forgiveness, and hope for God's coming Kingdom. The word "mission" describes our calling, while "theology" is the study of God. Together, missional theology examines God's nature and our role as participants in His mission.

As we grow as followers of Christ, we develop a deeper understanding of our role in sharing the Gospel, becoming the hands and feet of Jesus in our communities. For a long time, I assumed my primary role was to be a hospital and military chaplain, preaching, praying, and showing up in crisis. I learned how to notice where God is already at work in ordinary places: in conversations at the barn, in the way a therapy visit with Winston softened a hardened expression, or in the everyday kindness exchanged at our front door when someone dropped off a dog for boarding. My sense of "ministry" expanded from formal chaplaincy to a daily, place-based partnership in God's mission, where caring for the land and its neighbors became ways of being the hands and feet of Jesus.

We need to ask ourselves: What do we have that is*n't* a gift from God, including our pets or even the birds singing outside our windows? These creatures are precious gifts, and recognizing them encourages us to share our gift of life with others. Additionally, doing so highlights the diversity and creativity of God's love. By sharing our stories of experiencing God in the human and other-than-human world, we can testify to God's creativity and care for creation.

Central to this is the *missio Dei*, which emphasizes God's initiative in faith communities and highlights God's inherently missionary nature. When God sent His Son into the world, it was a missional act; as when Jesus sent His disciples, it was, too. Today, that same sending reaches all the way down into the hidden places of our own lives, namely our hearts, minds, and wills. The *missio Dei* does not begin "out there" in programs or strategies; it begins as we offer our own will to God and consent to be formed as intentional participants in His reconciling work. In the practices of prayer, Scripture meditation, examen, and daily discernment, we learn to attend to God's presence and to align our desires with His. As this interior posture deepens, we grow into a missional mindset, so that being "sent" is not merely an activity of the Church but a way of inhabiting every context of our lives. Missional theology is therefore not just church theory; it is a profoundly practical way of the spiritual life, as the Spirit guides us to live out God's mission in our particular places and callings. When we recognize that God's mission includes the entire created order, even these interior practices begin to reshape how we relate to others, drawing us into our participation in the *missio Dei*.

BECOMING MINDFUL PARTICIPANTS IN GOD'S MISSION

We cannot predict or control when God will break through to our spirits, and it often happens in unlikely moments: a grazing muzzle in a barn, attentive deer on a wooden path, a leashed miniature donkey in a hospital corridor. Yet God gives us real agency to participate in our own healing and growth. God works with us to examine our nets, notice their shortcomings, and repair, rebuild, or replace them. It is through the willing cooperation that we create space for God's work within us.

Refining our nets involves examining how our assumptions, biases, and cultural backgrounds influence our understanding of God's mission. This process calls for humility, openness to mystery, and a willingness to let God's reality reshape our frameworks. One way to achieve this is to seek out diverse voices and experiences, and to listen to those who differ from us, including people from different cultures and backgrounds. These perspectives can reveal aspects of God's work that our current nets might overlook.

For example, if our framework overemphasizes rationality or perfection, we might dismiss deeply felt experiences as "merely subjective" or even ungodly. A megachurch attendee might see a decisive moment during worship as something unique to their tradition, or even as a reward for regular attendance, rather than recognizing that moments of awakening and encounter can happen across different traditions and spiritual practices. In other words, the attendee has genuinely experienced God, but their perspective may prevent them from seeing how broadly God's Spirit moves.

By staying open to God's presence in unexpected places, people, and creatures, we start to see that God's truth and activity are not limited to our narrow views.

As we allow God to refine our nets, we may find ourselves drawn more deeply into the *missio Dei*, participating not only in the reconciliation of human beings to God but also in restoring the connections within the GHAB.

REMEMBER THAT WE ARE ANIMALS, TOO

Let's start by making sure we're on the same page: We are animals and part of the animal kingdom, too. Although this is scientifically clear, we often act and speak as if we are somehow more divine than other mammals.

One humid summer evening, I was refilling the dogs'

water bowls after a long day. As I stood at the sink, I noticed how automatic the motion had become: turn on the tap, fill the bowl, set it down. My dogs trotted over, drank the cool water, and then lay down with a satisfied sigh. A little later, I grabbed my own bottle of water from the counter, took a long drink, and felt the same relief wash over me.

It was such an ordinary scene that I almost missed what it revealed. Simply, we were thirsty creatures, each finding our way to the same basic gift of water. There was no hierarchy, just bodies needing water, and made by the same God. Remembering that I, too, am an animal does not diminish my humanity; it deepens my sense of kinship and responsibility. It reminded me that to participate in God's mission is, in part, to recognize and honor this shared creatureliness.

In academic and ethical conversations, a more precise term than simply "animals" is "other-than-human animals."[4] This language recognizes humans as a single species within the broader animal kingdom. It helps distinguish us from other species without placing us outside creation. I appreciate what this phrase is trying to do (even though it's cumbersome). It challenges the idea that humans are separate from all living creatures, reminding me that I, too, am an animal. In everyday speech, I usually say "animals," but I keep "other-than-human animals" in the back of my mind as a helpful reminder.

As you read, I invite you to treat words like "human," "animal," and even "other" with care. My goal isn't to create a hierarchy that puts humans at the top and views other species as inferior, as if they were just our footstool. I want to depict relationships among God, humans, and animals without a vertical ranking.

In the following sections, I offer practical, theological, and missional reflections on how humans and other-than-human animals live together in God's world.

Over time, I have come to see that creatures are not just background details in our faith stories; they are part of the setting in which those stories unfold.

GROCERY STORE PARKING LOT

One afternoon at the grocery store, I found myself hurrying toward the entrance, mentally making a list of everything I needed to buy. As I pushed my cart across the parking lot, a sparrow hopped along the painted white line beside me, pecking at crumbs someone had dropped. I almost missed her. Cars idled, doors slammed, a shopping cart clattered against a corral, and right there, this tiny bird hopped around searching for her daily bread.

I stopped for a moment, resting my hands on the cart. Instead of seeing a "background bird," I saw a fellow creature, part of the same creation I had just rushed past. Her presence pulled me out of my hurry and into a brief moment of shared existence. In that parking lot, between sliding doors and sale signs, I sensed the nudge of the Spirit: Remember, you are not the only one God is feeding today. Pay attention to the other creatures who share this world with you.

RESTAURANT PATIO

One day, Jenny and I met a friend for lunch at a restaurant with outdoor seating. As we walked in together, my body shifted into that familiar high-alert mode. I became suddenly aware of how close we were standing, how easily someone might read us as a couple, even without seeing us hold hands. I found myself subtly adjusting the space between us, scanning the room to see who glanced our way, whose eyes lingered a little too long, and whose smile was a bit too tight. We were just two women going to lunch, but I still caught myself wondering, If they know she's my spouse, will they see us differently? Will we be welcomed in the same way?

We sat down and settled into conversation. A few minutes later, a brown service dog trotted past our table, vest on, tail wagging slowly. He glanced in our direction, nose sniffing the air thick with grilled food, then tipped his head up to catch the eye of his handler, as if to ask, "Is this safe? Are we okay here?" His ears were forward, his steps steady and close to his handler's leg, not frantic, not loose, but his focus told me that he had been trained to stay near and pay attention.

I felt a tug of recognition. The service dog was doing, in his own way, what I had just done when Jenny and I walked onto the patio, reading the space and looking for signs of welcome or warning. Watching him navigate the noise of clinking dishes, rolling carts, and human conversation, I sensed how similarly we experience the world, despite our vast differences. He relies on his handler to guide and protect him in a world that rarely feels predictable. In a very real way, I'm invited to place that same trust in God's presence with me, even when I'm unsure how others will respond to my wife and me.

Between bites of our sandwiches and sips of iced tea, the restaurant patio became a gathering place, a reminder that "the other" walks beside us, often unnoticed, sharing our streets, our questions, our fears, and our hopes. Seeing myself and Jenny as "the other" helped me view this service dog not just as background or equipment, but as a neighbor in God's creation, also navigating belonging and safety in a world that isn't always kind.

Experiences like these gradually reshape how I interpret Scripture and understand God's mission in the world. They also influence how I teach, pray, and counsel: I mention sparrows, deer, and other overlooked creatures in sermons, prayers, and moments of counsel, to help others see that God's mission unfolds not only in sanctuaries but also in parking lots, driveways, patios, and fields.

SCRIPTURE, MISSION, AND FORMATION

Experiencing God's movement in the world and in our lives is deeply mysterious. The Psalms provide poetic testimony to God's initiative and constant presence, affirming that mission always starts with divine action, which then invites human cooperation. God's presence itself is an act of sacred initiative, and when we willingly align ourselves with God's purposes, we become part of His ongoing work. In this way, faithful spiritual practices are crucial; in fact, they prepare and shape us as vessels to be filled.

Greg McKinzie, whose research focuses on biblical interpretation at the intersection of mission and theology (missional hermeneutics), argues that our purpose and mindset as readers significantly influence our approach to the Bible.[5] He explains that merging theology and mission is not just theoretical; it shapes our understanding of how the Bible impacts our identity and sense of mission in the world. What we believe, how we think, and the habits we develop shape our interpretation of Scripture, and that interpretation, in turn, reshapes our beliefs, practices, and sense of calling as participants in God's mission.

I strongly connect with this take on mission and interpretation, and I see it clearly reflected in my own experiences. When I regularly read and meditate on passages such as Genesis 2, Psalm 104, or Proverbs 12:10, texts that speak of shared creatureliness and vocation to "till and keep," of God's generous provision and of righteousness expressed in caring for the needs of animals, I notice that my beliefs and attitudes toward animals are reoriented.

This reorientation, therefore, guides my actions: I show

more kindness toward animals, support animal welfare initiatives, and advocate for responsible environmental stewardship. These experiences, in turn, deepen my understanding of Scripture and reinforce my belief in how the *missio Dei* is practically lived. Belief and practice are organic, and the Spirit continues to reshape them so that we may reimagine servant roles to the rest of creation.

When we search the Bible in light of the *missio Dei*, we often encounter active verbs such as "create," "form," "sustain," and "redeem." I'm not claiming that any single verse proves a cosmic *missio Dei* on its own; rather, I'm reading these texts together as part of Scripture's wider pattern in which God's creative, sustaining, and reconciling work always reaches beyond humanity to embrace the whole creation. These words often highlight God's ongoing, active role in creation and history, emphasizing that mission begins with God's initiative and that this initiative is far greater than human souls.

Once we notice that the biblical narrative portrays God as active and present in creation, we not only gain insight into God's mission but also come to embody it. This transformation touches every part of our lives, our communities, and our relationships. It is through faithful Scripture reading and interpretation, responding to a calling, prayer, and the willingness to serve that we become partners in God's ongoing work of reconciliation.

THE FOUNDATION OF A MISSIONAL MINDSET

If I could hold all the spiritual practices in my hand and squeeze them in my fist, I'm sure that the two greatest commandments would drip out: to love God with all my heart, soul, and mind, and to love my neighbor as myself (Matt. 22:37–39). This is the spiritual foundation of everything, including this book: The God *who is* Love is *the heart of the mission*. Our words, actions, and disciplines are meaningful and transformative only when rooted in love. Love does not hesitate; it moves toward God, neighbors, and creation. This love turns simple rituals into genuine acts of care and devotion.

Ultimately, spiritual practices and sacraments, whether discernment, prayer, social justice, or baptism and communion, can be considered missional when they *originate from and aim toward* loving God and loving others. Of course, spiritual practices can be *transformative experiences*, even when we don't feel motivated to do them or can't seem to "feel" the love in them. Participating in these practices, regardless, can shape our hearts and lives. But honest self-reflection, genuine sincerity, and humble submission to God's guidance expand spiritual practices from items on a checklist to living expressions of God's mission through us. When driven by love, these acts shape not only what we do but also who we are as followers of Christ.

A THERAPY VISIT WITH WINSTON

I began to experience the GHAB as a love-rooted way of practicing faith in God's mission through my visits with Winston and the people we met. As part of a therapy team, before each visit to a hospital, a counseling center, AAI, or a workplace wellness event, I pause in the parking lot or barn and simply pray, "God, guide my intentions. Help me to love well today." I check Winston's halter, brush the dust from his coat, and make sure his hooves are clean, not just as routine care, but as an act of preparation. These ordinary movements are a kind of liturgy that prepares my heart to pay attention.

Inside the building, Winston often walks ahead of me with a calm, steady pace, and sometimes I can hear his breath. His hooves clop, clop on the floor, and I watch as people's faces soften when they see him: a nurse who has just finished a long, exhausting shift relaxes in her chair; a patient who hasn't smiled all week, finally grins; a family member carrying a grief they haven't put into words feels like sharing. Winston leans in for a nuzzle, breathing a comforting warmth on them, or simply stands still, looking at everyone. I don't say much, sometimes just, "Would you like to pet him?" And then I listen and watch.

In those encounters, I sense that more is happening than a mere visit from a cute animal. The GHAB becomes a living practice: God's love flowing through my intention to serve, Winston's steady body and calm spirit, and the open heart of the one God has brought into our path.

Nothing about these visits is flashy. There are no sermons, no microphones, no altar calls, only presence and a shared breath. These visits have a missional impact because they are empowered by love, a love that begins in God, that flows between Winston and me, and that expands outward through the presence we share to bring comfort, peace, and hope to others. In the bigger picture, Winston and I are simply participating in what God is already doing.

HOLY LINKS: ANIMALS, PRESENCE, AND A CHAIN OF KINSHIP

Many people report that animals comfort them during times of suffering, offering companionship and peace when words fall short. I think of a woman in hospice whose dog lay pressed against her side during her last days, breathing very slowly as she slept. The medical staff checked her vitals and adjusted medications, but it was the steady weight of his body and the rhythm of his breath that seemed to calm her most. He did not fix anything;

he was simply there. This kind of comfort echoes what chaplains call a "ministry of presence." Often, we simply sit with someone in distress, perhaps holding a hand or sharing silence, and that uncomplicated act becomes a powerful reminder of God's caring presence.

Animals, too, provide this ministry of presence in their own way. A cat curling beside a lonely person or a therapy animal leaning into a hospital bed are all silent and sacred reminders that we are not alone. These moments can be called "Holy Links" in the omnipresent chain of God's love.

This imagery of Holy Links helps me picture how God's love forms an eternal, lateral, unbreakable chain of communion. Each act of presence, comfort, or kindness, whether through a chaplain, a friend, or an animal, serves as a sacred link, empowered by the Holy Spirit, symbolizing God's unwavering commitment to His creation. No matter how many links are added or how far apart we may feel from one another, this living chain of relationship endures, because the Spirit, not because any hierarchy of value, holds it together.

Whenever we show genuine compassion, offer forgiveness, or simply share a moment of attentive presence, the Holy Spirit is at work, binding our hearts not only to other humans but to all living things. In this way, these connections are not just figures of speech but spiritual realities, moments when the Spirit's activity makes visible the otherwise invisible bonds that hold creation together. When I say "metaphor," I simply mean using one image to help us understand something else. This symbolic image of chain links reminds us that, at the heart of all this, is God's relentless pursuit of a relationship, and that He gives *every* animal its being. Recognizing these links already places one within the realm of Christian mysticism, where God's presence is felt rather than analyzed.

Karl Rahner, the Jesuit theologian, once wrote, "the devout Christian of the future will either be a 'mystic,' one who has 'experienced' something, or will cease to be anything at all."[6] The term "mystic" might sound intimidating, but at its core, it simply means someone who has experienced God. This resonates with me because the most life-changing moments in my own journey with God have been encounters I cannot fully explain, yet that have clearly shaped my life.

THE BALANCE OF ACTION AND CONTEMPLATION

To live out a missional mindset, we need to find a rhythm between doing and being, between serving others and nurturing our inner lives. To be coworkers in God's mission, we need to practice love through both silence and action.[7] Silence in God's presence cultivates authenticity and responsiveness to God's purpose.

An exclusively active lifestyle, devoid of stillness, can lead to compassion fatigue, stress, and burnout. Silence allows us to hear God's voice more clearly. Silence and stillness also possess healing qualities, shifting us from stress to restoration. In our overstimulating world, practices of stillness are vital for mental and emotional well-being.

John 20:21 is tattooed on the inside of my right wrist as a daily reminder to go, walk, share, listen, and engage. I'm called to reflect God's love to all the people, animals, plants, and ecosystems of creation. Psalm 46:10, "Be still, and know that I am God," is tattooed on the inside of my left wrist as a daily reminder to cultivate stillness, contemplation, imagination, wonder, and rest in God's Holy presence. I'm called to bask in God's steadfast and eternal love for me. Both active engagement (doing) and contemplative stillness (being) are vital for faithful discipleship.

ARCHIMEDES' LEVER AND EMBRACING THE ANIMALS

It is ironic that silence and stillness generate power. Think of a lever and a fulcrum as symbols of God's mission in the world. Archimedes reportedly said, "Give me a place to stand, and I will move the earth."[8] In life, the Holy Spirit is the force that moves the lever, while God's steady presence is the foundation beneath our feet, the place to stand. It is in the very moment of our intention that we must grasp the lever, lean our weight into it, and move it with sweat and hard work. Our commitment to stand with the Spirit and take responsibility for our role in the world is the starting point of being intentional.

One of the most significant ways we choose where to stand and how to lean our weight into God's mission is by deciding who counts as our neighbor. A core element of having a missional mindset is expanding our circle of compassion to include *the other*, including animals. Recognizing animals as *the other* challenges us to extend empathy and solidarity beyond human boundaries. How do our relationships with animals mirror the love, compassion, stewardship, and interconnectedness that are central to the gospel?

The human–animal relationship often fits into binary categories: us versus them, strong versus weak, valuable versus expendable. It is up to us, as moral agents, to recognize and resist this binary language, which can help us move past a mindset of separation and superiority, cultivating a deeper sense of unity. In my own life, learning to see animals as neighbors and friends has transformed my view of stewardship and mission-driven living.

Our shared experience is reflected in the ways we interact, learn, and grow together. The Holy Spirit connects us to God, to one another, and to creation. Our shared story is the narrative of creation itself. The wonder we share with animals emerges in moments of mystery and presence.

Ultimately, the Kingdom of God is the eternal hope, where God's love and justice reign supreme, drawing creation into healing and renewal. Sharing our God–human–animal stories fosters transformation, especially when we bring new perspectives to familiar experiences. This book aims to do just that: weave creation stories and personal faith journeys, including animal stories, into a series of links that form holy connections.

Psalm 104 portrays a world in which all creation is the Lord's handiwork, and the living thrive through God's sustenance and provision. Our gifts, whether practical or spiritual, are intended to advance the Kingdom. Even simple acts of farming, dog boarding, and walking a dog become ministries when done out of love.

In these everyday moments, we have the chance to pause, notice creation, and marvel at the wonders God provides. This is the Holy Link of the GHAB: our relationships with animals become places where God's love is revealed, shared, and embodied.

As we pay closer attention to God's presence within and around us, we realize that spiritual reflection and physical activity both become pathways for experiencing and embodying God's grace. Attentiveness to the Spirit transforms ordinary experiences into opportunities for growth and engagement in God's mission.

In the end, Archimedes' metaphorical lever offers a vivid image of the life of faith. God has already given us a place to stand—in Christ. The question is *how* we will lean the weight of our lives *into that place*. When we choose to stand with the Spirit and extend our love to animals as well as humans, the lever begins to move. The earth may not shift suddenly, but certain places become fulcrum points where the Kingdom of God leans in. There, in the GHAB, we begin to glimpse what it means for all creation to be drawn into the reconciling love of God.

QUESTIONS FOR REFLECTION AND PRACTICE

- Think about your own pets, working animals, or other animals in your neighborhood. What changes when you ask, *"What if these bonds are not just 'extra,' but part of how God is already reaching me and others?"*
- This week, choose *one* regular interaction with an animal, and intentionally *hold it* before God in prayer. How does viewing that relationship as part of the *missio Dei* and the GHAB affect the way you speak, act, or give thanks in that moment?

NOTES

1. Pet Partners, Pet Partners Therapy Animal Program: Policies and Procedures (Bellevue, WA: Pet Partners, 2017), accessed January 26, 2026, *https://petpartners.org/wp-content/uploads/2023/06/PoliciesProceduresTAP_2017-rebranded.pdf.*
2. Amanda Gefter, "Finding Peter Putnam," Nautilus, accessed October 27, 2023, *https://nautil.us/finding-peter-putnam-1218035/.*
3. Gefter, "Finding Peter Putnam."
4. Laura Hobgood-Oster, Holy Dogs and Asses: Animals in the Christian Tradition (Urbana: University of Illinois Press, 2008).
5. Greg McKinzie, Hermeneutics of Participation (Eugene, OR: Cascade Books, 2021), 5.
6. Karl Rahner, "Christianity of the Future," in Concern for the Church: Theological Investigations XX (New York: Crossroad, 1981), 149. In full, Rahner writes: "It has already been pointed out that the Christian of the future will be a mystic or he will not exist at all. To further clarify: 'if by mysticism we mean, not singular parapsychological phenomena, but a genuine experience of God emerging from the very heart of our existence, this statement is very true, and its truth and

importance will become still clearer in the spirituality of the future."

7. Clemens Sedmak, Doing Local Theology (Maryknoll, NY: Orbis Books, 2003), 3–4. Engaging in theology, what Catholic theologian Clemens Sedmak calls doing theology, and practicing silence before God are both essential for meaningful participation as co-workers with God in the world.

8. "Give me a place to stand, and I will move the earth," is attributed to Archimedes, in The Oxford Dictionary of Quotations, 8th ed. (Oxford: Oxford University Press, 2014), s.v. "Archimedes."

2

A SHARED CONNECTION

While reading an issue of *Animal Frontiers*, I was captivated by how animal scientists describe our long, intertwined history with other creatures. Consider the centuries-old partnerships that have shaped and sustained both humans and other animals. David Magee and his colleagues, for example, trace the journey of cattle from their wild ancestor, the powerful aurochs, through multiple domestication events to the many breeds that sustain us today.[1] Through genetics and archaeology, their research shows how long we have relied on these animals and how closely their history is bound up with our own.

A similar pattern appears in our history with dogs. Marie-Pierre Horard-Herbin, Anne Tresset, and Jean-Denis Vigne describe how early interactions with dogs evolved from pure utility to spiritual significance.[2] During the Neolithic and later periods, dogs were not only companions but also bore symbolic roles, as seen in their burials alongside humans and their presence in ritual contexts. In many sites, dogs were treated as mediators or guardians in the afterlife. Their status rose beyond mere usefulness; they became protectors, guides, and messengers bridging mortal and divine realms. While we cannot know the beliefs of these ancient communities, the care invested in these burials suggests that dogs were regarded as more than tools or property, carrying social and even spiritual significance within human communities. This deep, long-standing pattern of honoring dogs as companions highlights what I call the GHAB, a sacred bond among God, humans, and animals.

Animal-assisted therapies, service animals, and equine-assisted activities are among the many ways animals support human emotional, physical, and mental well-being. The presence of animals is linked to improved health outcomes and greater independence for many people, underscoring a partnership built on trust, affection, and mutual benefit.

Our enduring bond with animals is also reflected in the reverence we show them. Dogs, in particular, are honored as loyal companions, protectors, and participants in rituals, ceremonies, and everyday expressions of gratitude. Their symbolic presence in art, literature, and spiritual practices has grown. These traditions, rooted in ancient beliefs, remind us that our connection with animals is both practical and deeply meaningful.

WHEN LOVE LINGERS AT THE DOOR

I see the same pattern in the lives of ordinary dog owners. A man dropping off his aging Labrador for boarding will often linger at the door, his hand resting on the dog's head a little longer than necessary. He might joke about the dog's slowing gait, but his eyes often reveal something deeper: gratitude for years of companionship and a fear of what it will mean to say goodbye, even if only for a short while. In those few seconds, the bond between them is not mere *theory*; it is a *lived experience*, carrying history, emotion, and mutual trust. Human–Animal Bond (HAB) research, which examines the measurable emotional and relational connections between people and animals, provides a language for describing what is occurring. Though for many people, it is simply love, a love that, in the language of this book, is central to the GHAB.

In the last four decades, the study of the HAB has emerged as a vital field of inquiry, uncovering psychological, social, and even spiritual dimensions of our relationships with animals.[3] Early pioneers such as Leo Bustad and Michael McCulloch began using the term "human–animal bond" in the late 1970s, inspired by the deep attachment they observed between parents and children, a dynamic they believed also existed between people and animals.[4] Their work helped found the Delta Society (now Pet Partners), an organization dedicated to exploring the interconnections among humans, animals, and the environment.[5]

Dr. Alan Beck, a pioneer in HAB research and founding director of Purdue University's Center for the Human–Animal Bond, has further advanced our understanding of HAB through his leadership of the Center.[6] Under his guidance, the Center has conducted empirical research on how contact with animals influences human stress, loneliness, and overall health, providing pastors, clinicians, and policymakers with data to support what many have long sensed anecdotally about the benefits of the HAB.

From a theological standpoint, the Center's work aligns with the belief that the HAB is part of a divinely designed order. Inspired by Larry Anderson's sculpture *Continuum* at Purdue University, *Continuum*[7] can be seen as a visual parable of God's intentionality in creation, reminding us that we are meant to coexist. Read alongside this, passages such as Genesis 2:19–20, where God brings animals to Adam to see what he will name them, and Psalm 104, which declares, "How many are your works, Lord! In wisdom you made them all; the earth is full of your creatures" (v. 24), and then prays, "When you hide your face, they are terrified; when you take away their breath, they die and return to the dust. When you send your Spirit, they are created, and you renew the face of the ground" (vv. 29–30).

Together, these texts emphasize the sacredness of all living beings and humanity's responsibility to nurture and protect them.

I sometimes imagine a golden dove as an eighth piece in the *Continuum*, hovering above the scenes as a symbol of peace, godly inspiration, and the breath of life within the human–animal relationship.[8] It would visually affirm that this bond is both a gift and a calling.[9]

Researchers often refer to the HAB to describe measurable, observable connections between people and animals. In this book, I use the term *GHAB* to describe how God's presence and love move within and through that bond.

At the same time, the HAB is not simple or always positive. Not every interaction with an animal is healing: some people live with allergies or phobias, some have been bitten or traumatized, and even well-loved animals can experience stress, overwork, or burnout in therapeutic settings. Remembering these limits keeps us from romanticizing the bond and invites us to practice interspecies ministry ethically. It means paying attention to the needs and boundaries of both humans and animals, prioritizing mutual well-being over the use of animals as tools.

SACRED CONNECTIONS

Many scholars, including those affiliated with Purdue's Center, recognize that the HAB is a distinct field encompassing behavioral, psychological, physiological, ecological, social, and ethical dimensions; yet the spiritual dimension is often overlooked. This book aims to name that dimension by attending to the Holy Spirit's work within the GHAB and by reflecting on stories and pastoral practices that make that work visible. In the language of Psalm 104, we confess, "How many are your works,

Lord! In wisdom you made them all; the earth is full of your creatures" (v. 24), and we pray, "When you hide your face, they are terrified; when you take away their breath, they die and return to the dust. When you send your Spirit, they are created, and you renew the face of the ground" (vv. 29–30). The same Spirit who gives us breath and renews the earth is the One we are learning to recognize in the bonds we share with animals.

The interactions we have with animals are meaningful because they shape both parties. Our growing appreciation for animals and their many roles in human life underscores the significance of this bond. Genuine relationships are not one-sided; they involve reciprocal benefit and importance for all involved.

My own understanding of this sacred connection deepened when I began serving with my dogs in hospice and hospital settings.

My Miniature Schnauzer and I became a therapy team in 2009 with the Delta Society, now Pet Partners. Learning how to be ministry partners built a strong bond of trust between us, enabling us to provide companionship and comfort to others. Before that, I had already taken another Miniature Schnauzer on hospice visits, offering presence and a calming influence for those in need, yet to have the support of an organization that recognized our skills and ministry felt like a gift and a commissioning.

One visit in particular stays with me.

PSI'S COMFORTING PRESENCE

We took the elevator to a hospice unit at a regional medical center to visit a patient. As I approached the door with my small dog, Psi, I saw a group of people gathered in the hallway, tears flowing down their faces as they spoke in hushed tones. I introduced myself, saying, "Hi,

I'm the hospice chaplain, and this is my dog, Psi." Their eyes widened, and one of them said, "Please, come on in," inviting me into the room of a woman I had never met.

Inside, three family members stood by the bedside of a woman who was in her final days. My first thought was, *this might not be the best time to bring my dog,* and a wave of panic washed over me. Psi, after all, was a symbol of joy and life, hardly what one might expect in such a somber moment. I introduced myself and apologized for bringing her, then began explaining that I had never met their loved one.

Then something unexpected happened.

As I set Psi down, the family members began to stroke her fur. Their hands moved rhythmically, almost as if they were drawing strength from her. They were crying and shaking their heads, yet their touch was tender, nearly reverent. Psi became a receptive vessel for their grief, absorbing and holding it with her steady presence. One woman whispered, "I'm so glad you brought your dog today; I needed her more than you know."

Standing there with an almost lifeless body before me, I realized I was on sacred ground. Psi and I were engaged in something more profound than words. We were doing theology without a single formal prayer or hymn. In that moment, I understood how some of the most profound acts of ministry happen in silence, in presence, in the unspoken language between humans and animals, and in the leading of the Holy Spirit.

Only later did I realize that these experiences were not just ministry in the moment but also preparation for a broader calling: to provide this kind of interspecies ministry, pastoral care that intentionally involves animals to more people, and to see it as part of God's larger mission.

A MYSTERIOUS CONNECTION

Why call the connection among God, people, and animals mysterious? Because it runs deeper than we can fully explain, it is a sacred bond between the Creator, us, and the creatures around us. It is like an invitation to pay attention and to see God's presence in everyday moments: a sparrow's chirp, a dog's sigh, a shared silence. This connection encourages us to live with gratitude and care for the world, finding meaning in the simple, ordinary things all around us.

Mysticism, at its core, is about being opened and transformed by God in the midst of ordinary life. For many of us, that ordinary life includes dogs and other animals. Our moments with the Holy will naturally include them, if we let them.

Early Christian mystics taught that God's presence is not limited to grand miracles or formal rituals. It can be discovered in subtle connections, for example, sitting still long enough to hear the buzz of hummingbird wings, or watching a fish glide back and forth in an aquarium and suddenly wondering how it knows how to swim. In such peaceful, grace-filled moments, we recognize that our wondrous God is the One who gives the hummingbird its wings and the fish its instinct to swim.

Spiritual practices can help us become more attentive to this presence. Finding a place, setting an intention to be mindful of the Spirit, and noticing our breath as a gift from God are meaningful steps. Including a pet in that contemplative moment, such as *drawing* a dog or cat close while you pray or rest, can become a simple, welcoming act and even a form of worship, honoring the Creator of both of you.

Even if you do not have an animal at home, you can imagine one that has been meaningful to you, or even an animal from a story. If you are able, step outside and listen to the birds during your prayer time. These creative acts open us to the possibility that God's voice, love, and comfort might come to us through the creatures who share our lives.

As we continue to explore in greater detail how spiritual practices can give us a deeper sense of interconnectedness with all creation, we begin to be drawn closer to the heart of God's ongoing work in the world, the *missio Dei* that reaches *through* the GHAB.

QUESTIONS FOR REFLECTION AND PRACTICE

» When you think about the long history of cattle, dogs, and other animals living alongside us, how does it change the way you see your own relationships with animals today? Do you sense that God might be at work in those bonds as part of a much bigger story?

» This week, pay attention to *one* recurring interaction you have with an animal. How might you recognize that moment as part of the GHAB? Or, perhaps, offer a brief prayer of thanks, a warm greeting, or an act of kindness.

NOTES

1. David A. Magee, David E. MacHugh, and Ceiridwen J. Edwards, "Interrogation of Modern and Ancient Genomes Reveals the Complex Domestic History of Cattle," *Animal Frontiers* 4, no. 3 (2014): 7–22.
2. Marie-Pierre Horard-Herbin, Anne Tresset, and Jean-Denis Vigne, "Domestication and Uses of the Dog in Western Europe from the Paleolithic to the Iron Age," *Animal Frontiers* 4, no. 3 (2014): 23–31.
3. Steven A. Zinn and Alan M. Beck, "From the Editors: The

Human–Animal Bond and Domestication: Through the Ages … Animals in Our Lives," *Animal Frontiers* 4, no. 3 (July 2014): 5–6, *https://doi.org/10.2527/af.2014-0016.*

4. Linda M. Hines, "Historical Perspectives on the Human–Animal Bond," *American Behavioral Scientist* 47, no. 1 (2003): 7–15, *https://doi.org/10.1177/0002764203255206.*
5. Hines, "Historical Perspectives on the Human–Animal Bond," 9.
6. Alan M. Beck, "The biology of the human–animal bond, *Animal Frontiers* 4, no. 3 (July 2014): 32–36, *https://doi.org/10.2527/af.2014-0019.* Accessed July 1, 2023.
7. Center for the Human–Animal Bond, "About the Continuum," College of Veterinary Medicine, Purdue University, accessed October 27, 2023, *https://www.vet.purdue.edu/chab/about/continuum.php.*
8. The dove is an early biblical symbol of an animal's involvement in the GHAB. As a ritually clean bird, unlike the raven (Gen 8:6), it could be included among the "burnt offerings from every clean animal and every clean bird" that Noah offers after the flood (Gen 8:20). The text does not specify whether the dove that returned with the olive leaf (Gen 8:11) was among those offered, and we cannot know. What we do know is that the dove's role in signaling the end of the flood and its being a clean animal suitable for sacrifice together demonstrate how a nonhuman creature can be both an agent of God's mercy and grace and a carrier of life-giving knowledge to humans, and can participate in covenantal worship.
9. The golden dove mentioned in the text is a symbolic addition by the author for theological reflection and is not part of Larry Anderson's original sculpture.

3

A SHARED LAND

In this chapter, I share a perspective on the God–Human–Animal Bond (the GHAB) as a Spirit-shaped bond among God, humans, and other animals that takes shape on the land we share. Land is not just a backdrop to our relationships; it is part of the bond itself. The ground is not God, but it is a place where God's presence and purposes are revealed. The same soil that grows our food also grows hay for animals. Hooves and paws follow the same paths we walk. Talking about the GHAB means talking about the land we share. The psalms remind us, "How many are your works, Lord! In wisdom you made them all; the earth is full of your creatures" (Ps. 104:24). Our shared land is a part of that creature-filled earth, shaped by God's wisdom.

My own stories unfold on forty rural acres, but the GHAB is not limited to farms and fence lines. While my bond with Winston is rooted in those forty acres, the GHAB does not require a farm; it requires a willingness to pay attention. A shared patch of land might be a backyard, a city park, a balcony with potted plants, or even a stretch of sidewalk where pigeons, sparrows, and neighbors cross paths. The point is *not* acreage but *the depth of attention: wherever creatures and people share time and space, that area can become part of the bond where God is working.*

WINSTON'S WORLD

Winston's paddock covers just over half an acre and is thoughtfully designed to mimic desert conditions. Despite this, lush green grass often appears, adding a splash of surprise and vibrancy to his space. He loves munching on a few sprigs here and there, as if he's at a salad bar. Although he enjoys foraging behind the barn or nibbling on hay in his stall, most of his time is spent in his paddock, which feels like his living room, a place where he can relax as comfortably as you or I would in our favorite recliner.

In the evenings, I bring him into the barn for safety and comfort. Winston also spends time in the backyard with the dogs, and, on special occasions, he's even been inside the house. To keep him mentally, physically, and emotionally engaged, we take three or four walks each week, either along the rural country roads or on a mowed path around the pasture behind our house. One perimeter walk covers about a quarter of a mile.

Although this place is often called Winston's world, our dogs and the dogs we board also share this land. We walk them along the same path that winds past Winston's paddock, following the Stations of the Cross mounted on the fence posts. As we move from station to station, with the animals padding beside us, we sometimes glance over at our neighbor's vineyard behind our property. At the point in the path where Jesus is depicted carrying the Cross, the vineyard comes fully into view. That meeting of animals, land, and the Passion story has become very meaningful to me: a reminder that, in that moment, it felt as if Christ's suffering and the love that carried it were reaching beyond the human story, across species and soil, touching the lives of those who walked across it.

During these outings, I point out the daffodils, the two willow oaks, and the mulberry trees Jenny and I planted, and I even sometimes have to redirect him when he decides a young sapling looks like a snack.

After our walks, we go back to the paddock because I know it's his special place. Still, if I have an extra minute, I make sure to spend time with him there afterward. Many mornings, even before sunrise, I sit in a camping chair and enjoy my coffee while he eats his small portion of vet-approved oatmeal, a simple routine we have settled on with moderation in mind. Whether I'm weeding, mowing, cleaning buckets, or stuffing his rubber ball with hay (a donkey-enrichment toy similar to a Kong for dogs), I'm always looking for ways to include him in my daily activities.

Sometimes, re-purposing an old milk jug gives us at least thirty minutes of entertainment and lots of fun. I fill a half-gallon jug with water, drop in apple slices, orange peels, and banana peels, and sprinkle a tiny pinch of oregano and Atlantic-harvested kelp on top, turning the jug into a puzzle-like challenge. (We use these treats sparingly and consult our vet, since donkeys are prone to metabolic issues.) Winston nudges, rolls, and paws at it, determined to free the treats inside. I've also laid out several large tarps on the ground so his world isn't just dirt and rocks, and under his overhang, there's a shatterproof mirror at his height so he can take a peek at himself now and then.

Obviously, these acts of enrichment are expressions of my love for him, and you wouldn't be the first to accuse me of spoiling him. But beneath the playfulness is something more serious: a desire to bridge the divide between species and to build a meaningful relationship in this particular patch of land we share.

It is on this ordinary ground that the sacred and our everyday lives meet. Just as God shows up in every corner of creation, I find myself drawn to Winston's paddock, looking for excuses to be present with him. What might seem like a simple enclosure becomes a world of its own. Winston's paddock is more than just a fenced space; it is a place where I linger, where I listen to his breathing, where I notice the way morning light hits his coat or how the wind moves through the trees beyond the fence. In many ways, this mirrors how God longs to be present with us, not out of obligation, but out of delight and love. I'm drawn to be with Winston in his familiar space, and reminded that God continually seeks to be with us in the ordinary places of our lives.

Our bond is literally rooted in that land. The same forty acres we walk, pray, and work on are the fields that grow the hay Winston eats. The hay we cut and bale from our property becomes his winter feed. The land that holds my footsteps also feeds him. His steady chewing under an open sky is a daily reminder that the GHAB is not just emotional; it is physical, ecological, and spiritual. We are both, in different ways, nourished by the same ground.

In Winston's world, then, the GHAB is enacted as shared presence and shared sustenance on a particular piece of earth, showing that our bond with animals is inseparable from the land that feeds and shelters us both.

A FRAGILE LIFE ON SHARED LAND

Sharing land with animals also means accepting their risks and sorrows. One spring, the cycle of new life was again visible in the birth of baby rabbits around the property. That same season, my dog Twig encountered a young rabbit in the backyard. In his instinctual play, he treated the rabbit like a toy, and it fled, clearly shaken. The next morning, as I entered Winston's stall to release him, he turned his head and looked intently behind him, as if trying to get my attention. There, tucked in a corner, was a tiny rabbit hiding nearby.

Wanting to help, I carefully scooped him up and moved him to a corner near the hay to rest without being disturbed. I set out a bowl of water and placed fresh herbs nearby, hoping he would find them and regain his strength. At the time, I did what I thought was best (Later, I learned that the recommended response in situations like this is to contact a licensed wildlife rehabilitator and minimize handling, both for the animal's safety and our own.) Even in my misplaced attempt to help, I was being taught how fragile wild lives are and how much care they require.

The following day, I checked on him, eager for a sign of recovery. Instead, I found his body lying lifeless among the untouched herbs and water. My grief was disproportionate, perhaps, to his size, but not to his worth in God's creation. Standing there in the barnyard, I was filled with questions about suffering and divine justice. Why such a defenseless creature? Why in my care and on this land we share?

I did not have answers. All I could do was become a messenger of what I had witnessed, sharing my sorrow with Jenny without rushing to explain it away. In that telling, something shifted. I began to see the little scene, a bed of hay, a circle of water and herbs, a little, lifeless body, as a kind of unintended altar, a tender echo of how Scripture speaks of honoring the dead and of hoping in resurrection.

I do not claim to understand exactly how this fits into God's work, but I trust that even this fragile life and our shared grief are held within God's larger movement toward renewal. This small tragedy made me wonder whether, in ways I cannot see, even our participation in suffering might be drawn into the *missio Dei*, God's mission to heal and redeem all of creation.

PORCHES AND OTHER PLACES AS SACRED GROUND

Closer to home, not all land is measured in acres. Sometimes it is as insignificant as a front porch.

During the early months of the COVID-19 pandemic, when much of life shrank to the size of a house and yard, many people found themselves paying new attention to the creatures sharing that limited space. One woman, undergoing cancer treatment in the Blue Ridge mountains, spent long hours on her front porch, too vulnerable to join the usual crowds and gatherings. There, on the edge of her property, a family of red-tailed hawks, cardinals, and hummingbirds became her unexpected companions.

Her porch became sacred ground, not because she had traveled somewhere extraordinary, but because God met her through the birds that claimed the air above her driveway and the trees. Her world had narrowed, but her attention had deepened. This common ground, even in miniature, became a place of encounter.

Our yards, balconies, and neighborhood sidewalks can be like that, too. Sometimes, they are the closest habitats we share with animals, the everyday spaces where we can start to see the GHAB at work, even if we have never set foot in a pasture.

If these rural outposts show the GHAB on a few acres, the mountain-side porch proves that liminal spaces, threshold places where the ordinary meets the sacred, can become sites where the GHAB comes to life.

THE LAND AS A LIVING WEB

These stories, Winston's paddock, a fragile rabbit by the hay barn, and a porch, remind us that forests, fields, and backyards are meaningful contexts, where the animals are playful, become afraid, and even lose their lives.

Pollinators, predators, scavengers, and decomposers are always at work in the soil and sky around us. Their hidden labor keeps the land habitable for us and for our animals. When we tend our forty acres, we are not just managing property; we are participating in a complex, God-sustained web of life.

If the GHAB involves a shared bond among God, humans, and animals, then the soil we occupy together is where that bond is enacted and most clearly seen. It is where hay grows, where rabbits hide, where donkeys rest, where birds nest, and where people walk, pray, and grieve.

Recognizing this living web prepares us to ask what it might mean to inhabit shared time and space faithfully before God. In other words, the living web of land and creatures is the organic context in which the GHAB becomes visible and where our participation in God's mission must be discerned.

LIVING FAITHFULLY AND PRACTICES OF CARE

Living faithfully also means recognizing the land's sacredness and vulnerability. It involves considering how our decisions, where we build, how we grow our apple trees, what we spray on the fields, and how we move through fields and forests, impact the other creatures that share this ground with us. It also means paying attention to how water moves across the ravines: noticing where heavy rains carve a temporary river through a low spot, and choosing a more level site for a new building so we do not disturb that water path or too much of the surrounding ground.

Sometimes, our efforts to care for "the dirt" may seem rather minor: planting native flowers for pollinators, leaving a brush pile for rabbits and birds, and choosing not to cut down a tree that shelters hawks. However, they can also take larger forms: protecting a pasture from overuse, advocating for a local watershed, or supporting conservation work beyond our own fence lines.

Most of our property-stewardship does not feel heroic. It looks like walking ditches with a trash bag.

THE ROADSIDE

For as long as we've lived here, we have been picking up litter along our rural roads. I have done it in various ways: sometimes with a dog harnessed to a cart, carrying a growing bag of cans and wrappers; sometimes with Winston on a lead, his long ears flicking as we move slowly along the gravel; sometimes driving our utility vehicle at a crawl, stopping every few yards to grab another bottle or plastic bag from the grass. Over time, Winston has learned to enjoy these slow, stop-and-go walks. We do this in daylight, wearing bright vests and staying on the shoulder, so that the animals and we remain visible and safe. Each time I pause to snag a plastic bag from the fence line, he happily drifts toward the trees to forage, as if trash signals a kind of fast food for extra foraging time. What interrupts my pace becomes, for him, another way to enjoy the land we are tending together.

In recent years, Jenny and I have participated in Marshall County's Solid Waste Management team for their twice-a-year community cleanup. They give us bright-orange vests, trash pickers, and heavy-duty bags, and then we, along with other volunteers, help clean up the county roads. After a morning of bending, reaching, and hauling, we all gather at Rock Creek Park in Lewisburg. One of the county commissioners stands at the grill, flipping burgers in a cloud of smoke, while people remove their safety vests and share stories about the strangest things they pulled from the roadside. Nearby, trucks wait with open beds so we can toss our bags in; later, the crews will weigh the load.

One year, Jenny and I kept track of our totals, adding up the numbers from official cleanups and our own walks along nearby roads. By the end of the year, we had removed more than three hundred pounds of trash from the ditches.

It is not glamorous work. No one cheers when we stop the utility vehicle to retrieve a faded cup from a culvert or when Winston and I pause our walk so I can fish out a candy wrapper from the tall grass. I understand that this land-sharing is not identical, but deeply connected before God. The roads we walk and drive on are not ours alone; they are corridors used by deer and dogs, hawks and rabbits, and by neighbors we may never meet. Clearing them is one way we participate in God's care for this place, keeping this stretch of earth a little more livable for every creature that uses it.

Each piece of trash we pick up from the roadside, in its own way, shows that the earth and animals matter, and, in essence, even the GHAB is worth caring for, one bag at a time. In the language of the psalms, "The earth is the Lord's, and everything in it, the world, and all who live in it" (Ps. 24:1). If creation mainly belongs to God, then our "caring" becomes our acts of service for the Lord. In these modest stewardship practices, the GHAB becomes sacramental living, as our care for the ground participates in God's ongoing care for all creatures.

QUESTIONS FOR REFLECTION AND PRACTICE

1. **For rural or suburban readers:** Where is your own "Winston's paddock," a place where you regularly linger with a creature (pet, livestock, or local wildlife)? What have you learned there about vulnerability, joy, or God's presence?
   » **For urban readers:** How does the "wild" show up in your life, such as on a balcony, in a courtyard, at a bus stop, or on a sidewalk? Which creatures share that space with you?

2. **For rural or suburban readers:** This week, take a slow "trash walk" along a road, at a field edge, or on a trail. Pray as you go. Notice how caring for that stretch of land, even in small ways, can become an act of worship.
   » **For urban readers:** Spend ten minutes one day this week watching a bird, squirrel, or insect in your neighborhood. Ask: What does this creature's daily life reveal about God's provision, creativity, or patience?
   » Recognizing that we live on common ground graciously provided by God is the first spiritual practice of care and reverence; the next is to continue to live diligently as if it really matters to other animals. I have reflected on land as the shared foundation for our lives, stories, and vocations. Next, we will shift from the broad concept of *shared land* to the more personal realm of *shared places:* specific locations where God, humans, and animals coexist, and where the GHAB is a lived, felt reality.

4

A SHARED PLACE

It may seem almost too obvious to say that God meets us in places, but where else could we encounter God except somewhere in creation, as in an actual room, on the ground, or in our hearts and minds? Still, we often overlook how deeply those somewheres shape how God's mission and the God–Human–Animal Bond (the GHAB) are lived.

I argue that place is not "behind the scenes" but an active participant in God's mission, and that the GHAB is embodied in particular locations where God's presence and human and animal lives meet. In this book, the GHAB names the living three-way relationship in which God, humans, and animals are bound together in creation, covenant, and redemption. This bond is never abstract; it takes shape in concrete places like homes, hillsides, temples, barns, and back roads, where our lives and the lives of animals are woven into God's ongoing work.

In this chapter, I use the word *"placeholder"* not to imply that animals are temporary or that places are disposable or easily replaced, but to describe tangible signs within and among creatures, locations, and material things that preserve space in our memory and imagination for God's continuous work. In this sense, places and the lives within them actively carry God's story forward, keeping these encounters from collapsing into the past.

With this in mind, we will first explore how certain Old Testament places function as temporary yet decisive sites of encounter. Then we will turn to the places that shape Jesus' life and ministry, where the GHAB comes into even sharper focus. Finally, we will trace how this "theology of place" touches our sense of home, our reading of history and sacrifice, and our everyday missional choices.

DISCOVERING GOD'S PRESENCE IN ORDINARY AND SACRIFICIAL PLACES

In our lives, the meaning and importance of places unfold in countless ways, whether in the comfort of childhood memories or the sacredness of ordinary life. Our earliest memories, like learning about God's creation with a beloved grandparent or caring for animals as a child, plant seeds of wonder and connection that grow throughout our lives. These simple foundational experiences shape our understanding of home and belonging and remind us that God is present in the places we live, both literal and symbolic. In their own way, these memories serve a function in our stories, iconic markers that help us remember how God has already met us in particular places.

As I read Scripture and listen to people's stories, my eyes and ears have been drawn to notice patterns, as if certain kinds of places keep rising to the surface. Scripture is filled with stories of place: from the wilderness (Matt. 4:1–11; Mk. 1:12–13) and the promised land (Gen. 12:1–7; Josh. 1:1–6) to the temple (1 Kgs. 8:10–13; Jn. 2:13–22), the nativity (Lk. 2:4–7), and the Garden of Gethsemane (Matt. 26:36–46; Mk. 14:32–42; Lk. 22:39–46; cf. Jn. 18:1). In these places, the created world is not merely an idea but an embodied reality: God formed humans from the ground, placed them among other creatures, and then entered that same creation. Through Christ, God began to restore the cosmos to himself. Each location marks a turning point or sacred encounter, showing that God meets people where they are, often transforming ordinary surroundings into holy ground. Similarly, our own lives are filled with places that become meaningful through our relationships and experiences.

All in all, these reflections show that place is not just a stage for props and characters. We do not grow in a vacuum. We grow within the ordinary places where we actually spend our days. Over time, certain places start to feel like home, not because they are inherently special, but because of what God does there and what we experience there, like meals shared, prayers whispered, animals cared for, grief carried, and joy received. In those physical settings, God uses repeated experiences, relationships, and memories to anchor us, stretch us, and teach us to trust him. Whether through the stories of Scripture, cherished memories, or time with a beloved animal, we are reminded that God meets us in every place, calling us to see the supernatural in the ordinary and to find belonging wherever love is shared. These are often the very places where the GHAB becomes most visible.

The biblical stories we have just traced are not meant to remain distant. In what follows, I turn to the kinds of places and memories in our own lives where God, humans, and animals meet in similar ways.

To see this more clearly, I begin with several "temporary places" in the Old Testament that open the way to Jesus' own ministry places.

TEMPORARY PLACES IN THE OLD TESTAMENT AND PATTERNS OF PLACE

MOSES' HEART AND THE BURNING BUSH

In Moses' encounter at the burning bush (Exod. 3), an ordinary patch of ground becomes "holy" because God speaks there. A simple desert hillside is transformed into a place of calling and commissioning. Moses is told to remove his sandals, not because the soil has changed in substance, but because God's presence has claimed that particular place for a specific purpose. This reminds us that God can turn seemingly overlooked locations, such as a rocky hillside with a single shrub, into a material reality that becomes a vehicle for God's self-communication.

Experiences like Moses' still occur in ways today. Many people can point to a pasture, a hospital room, a trail, or a barn where they sensed God's call or comfort, yet they may hesitate to name those moments as holy. Part of our task in this book is to recognize such encounters for what they are: places where God meets us through creation, including animals and the land, and invites us into the next step of the *missio Dei*. Retelling, rediscovering, and reimagining our place in this way is crucial for reimagining our own stories with all of God's creation. Even when animals are not named, the location itself acts as a created partner, reminding us that the GHAB is rooted in soil, shrubs, and sky before it is understood, known, or theorized.

NOAH'S HEART AND THE ARK

If God did not care about the places we live, Noah would not have been inspired by God to build an ark to save his family and two of every kind of animal (Gen. 6:19). The ark became a symbol of the place God provided: a temporary home and sanctuary for preserving humans and animals. Noah is described as "a righteous man, blameless among the people of his time" (Gen. 6:9). Although he is not a priest and does not come from a priestly line, he lives a life of covenant obedience: he builds the ark according to God's command (Gen. 6:14–16), waits on the Lord within that floating home (Gen. 8:13–14), and then offers burnt offerings when he emerges (Gen. 8:20).

One of the key verses in the flood story says, "But God remembered Noah and all the wild animals and the livestock that were with him in the ark, and he sent a wind over the earth, and the waters receded" (Gen. 8:1). The Hebrew word for "wind" here is the same *ruakh*, God's Spirit, "hovering over the waters" at the original creation story (Gen. 1:2). Over the floodwaters, as when "the Spirit of God was hovering over the waters" (Gen. 1:2), the *ruakh* moves again, nearly marking a second creation about to begin.[1] In this way, the ark is more than just a vessel for survival; it is a Spirit-imbued space where righteous human life and wild animals—both clean, suitable for sacrifice, and unclean, preserved to repopulate the earth—are kept together as the foundation of a new creation.[2] Here, the ark becomes a shared place where God's Spirit, humans, and animals ride out judgment together, a vivid early picture of the GHAB.

JONAH'S HEART AND THE WITHERING PLANT

On Jonah's journey, he was overwhelmed by emotion and fatigue as he sat beneath a gourd and fell asleep after witnessing Nineveh's repentance to God (Jon. 3:5–10). The plant is one place of encounter, but another is Jonah's own heart, where he is resistant to extending mercy, which he himself had received (cf. Jon. 2:1–9; 4:1–3). God withered the plant at a specific moment to confront Jonah's inner attitude (Jon. 4:5–11), revealing that the Spirit not only sends us to difficult places (cf. Jon. 1:1–3; Jn. 20:21–22; Acts 1:8) but also works within us to transform the unseen places, like our hearts, where we resist God's mercy (cf. Ezek. 36:26–27; Phil. 2:12–13).

Read alongside the animals who also share in Nineveh's repentance (Jon. 3:7–8), the story hints that even a shaded hillside and its creatures are drawn into God's patient reconciling work. These Old Testament scenes prepare us to see that God's mission will continue to unfold in concrete places where God, humans, and animals meet, most fully in the incarnate life of Jesus.

MEMORIES OF SACRED PLACES: THEOLOGICAL AND PRACTICAL MEANING

Before turning to Jesus' places, we need one more theological thread: how place and animals work together in memory and imagination.

In this context, I'm not treating animals as "placeholders" in a disposable or merely instrumental sense. Rather, in continuity with my earlier definition, animals themselves can function as *living placeholders*: tangible, embodied creatures whose presence in particular places keeps open a space in our memory and imagination for God's ongoing work. They serve as living markers of place and representatives of creation within the story of God's people, both historically and in our theological imagination. Together, places and the animals within them actively carry God's story forward, preventing these sacred encounters from fading into a distant past and instead drawing us back into the GHAB in the present.

Recognizing animals as living markers of place in our memories shapes how we reimagine animals' life and death, understand eternal reconciliation, and live out our interconnectedness within God's story. These sacred sites, and the animals within them, not only shape our understanding of God's story but also invite us to see how the natural world continues to connect with our daily lives. In many biblical narratives, animals and physical locations work together to reveal aspects of God's character and mission.

With this in mind, we now follow the incarnate footprints of Jesus, exploring how certain locations in his life reveal the GHAB and teach us to see our own places differently.

JESUS' PLACES: WHERE THE GHAB COMES INTO FOCUS

THE NATIVITY: A PLACE OF HUMBLE INCARNATION

The nativity shows God's decision to enter the world in a setting of poverty, vulnerability, and shared human life (Lk. 2:4–7; cf. 2 Cor. 8:9). Animals share the space with Christ's birth, as the Christian tradition has long imagined, even though Luke does not explicitly name them.[3] In this received imagery, God does not come from afar but as part of creation (cf. Lk. 2:7, 12, 16; Isa. 1:3). The stable becomes a kind of first sanctuary where straw, a manger, humans, and animals all gather around the incarnate Word (Jn. 1:14; Phil. 2:6–8).

This humble scene reveals that all creation is welcomed into the place of God's arrival, a place characterized by humility, hospitality, and the blending of the sacred with the everyday (Lk. 2:10–14; Col. 1:15–20). From a GHAB perspective, the nativity offers our first view of Jesus and animals sharing a close, intimate space. This shared place of straw, manger, and animal breath foreshadows a mission lived out among, and never above, other creatures.

THE WILDERNESS: A PLACE OF TESTING AND DEPENDENCE

In the wilderness, the Spirit guides Jesus to be "with the wild animals" (Mk. 1:13; cf. Lk. 4:1). The Greek word for "wilderness," *erēmia*, means "desolate" or "isolated," yet even there God is present. The wilderness becomes a place of testing, solitude, and radical dependence on the Father's provision, a setting where Jesus' identity as the beloved Son is tested but not broken.

Mark notes that Jesus was "with the wild animals." Some interpreters see this as highlighting the danger of the wilderness, others as a sign that creation stands with the Son.[4] Here, I read it in the latter sense, as an early glimpse of the GHAB. This detail is important and often overlooked. It shows that Jesus is not only among people but also among the animals. Even harsh and lonely landscapes can become places of encounter and transformation when God meets us there. Here, the GHAB is present: the Son of God stands within a creation that is both risky and beloved, sharing the wilderness with wild animals who bear the same harsh conditions and the same sustaining care of the Father.

THE MOUNTAINS: PLACES OF SOLITUDE, PRAYER, AND REVELATION

Mountains in Scripture often serve as liminal spaces, places where heaven and earth seem to draw closer together. Jesus frequently seeks out these high places for solitude and prayer, slipping away from crowds and demands to be alone with the Father (Lk. 5:16; 6:12). On a mountainside, he calls the disciples and appoints them as apostles (Mk. 3:13–15), indicating that vocational clarity often arises in spaces of withdrawal, silence, and attentive listening.

On another mountain, Jesus delivers what we now call the Sermon on the Mount, teaching his disciples about life in the kingdom of God (Matt. 5–7). Here, a hillside becomes a natural amphitheater and a classroom for discipleship. The landscape itself participates: picture the birds of the air and lilies of the field being drawn into his teaching as living examples of trust and divine care (Matt. 6:26–30). In this way, the mountain is not just a backdrop for doctrine but a shared space where creation, human community, and divine instruction come together.

Perhaps the most memorable mountain scene is the Transfiguration. Jesus takes Peter, James, and John up a high mountain where "his face shone like the sun, and his clothes became white as light" (Matt. 17:1–2; cf. Mk. 9:2–8; Lk. 9:28–36). Moses and Elijah appear, and a bright cloud overshadows them as God's voice declares, "This is my Son, whom I love; with him I am well pleased. Listen to him!" (Matt. 17:5). The mountain becomes a place of unveiled glory and affirmation, a reminder that the one who walks dusty roads and sits in fishing boats is also the radiant Son through whom all things were made (Jn. 1:3; Col. 1:16).

THE TEMPLE: A PLACE OF WORSHIP AND SACRIFICE

First, it should be noted that God is omnipresent (Ps. 139:7–10), yet he chooses to be present in specific places, as if he is especially available there or seeks to draw people into his presence. While God is present everywhere (Ps. 139:7–10), he also chooses to be especially present with his covenant people in particular places and to meet them in a distinct way in worship. Second, he does not necessarily adapt to our needs as much as he meets us in ways that, as finite creatures, we can best receive his Spirit.

Before a permanent temple was built in Jerusalem, people worshiped God in the tabernacle (Exod. 29:42–46), or tent of meeting, which served as a portable sanctuary where God promised to dwell and meet with them (Exod. 25–31; 35–40; 29:42–46). Solomon's temple in

Jerusalem, the first temple, was later rebuilt after the exile and then became the fixed, central place where heaven and earth met through worship, prayer, and sacrifice (1 Kgs. 6:1; 8:10–13; Ezra 3:10–13).

Animals played a central role in the sacrificial rituals, symbolizing atonement, gratitude, and covenant faithfulness (Lev. 1–7; Deut. 12:5–7). The environment was filled with awe and mutual reverence. However, it was probably not the most pleasant place for worshipers: the temple courts likely echoed with the sounds of animals and the strong smell of blood and smoke, even though God accepted those offerings as holy.

As evangelical New Testament author G. K. Beale argues, the Jerusalem temple was never meant to be an end in itself but a pointer to something larger: a micro-scale representation of God's cosmic temple, the whole creation designed for his glory.[5] Hebrews describes the earthly sanctuary as a "copy and shadow of what is in heaven" (Heb. 8:5), a sign pointing beyond itself to the heavenly temple where Christ now ministers as the High Priest (Heb. 8:1–2; 9:11–12, 23–24). God's dwelling is not limited to stone and courtyards; the Holy One worshiped in the heavenly sanctuary also chooses to meet us in ordinary places on earth. The temple, in this sense, is a vast architectural placeholder, preserving in stone and sacrifice a living memory of God's desire to dwell with all creation.

Within this framework, Jesus' presence in the temple, first as a child who lingers "in his Father's house," then as a teacher, re-centers this space around himself (Lk. 2:41–49; Jn. 2:13–22; Matt. 21:12–16). He embodies the meeting of heaven and earth that the temple was always meant to symbolize. The tabernacles and temples served as training grounds for us to recognize his "temple presence" in all creation.

From a GHAB perspective, the temple reminds us that God's covenant relationship has always involved more than just humans. Animals, sacrificial practices, and the very architecture of place are drawn into worship and reconciliation. Today, whenever we gather for worship, prayer, and acts of kindness, our lives become living offerings that reflect those sacred rhythms (Rom. 12:1; Heb. 13:15–16). Any place can become an outpost of God's cosmic temple, a corner of creation where the *missio Dei* and the GHAB come together.

THE SEA OF GALILEE: A PLACE OF CALLING, TEACHING, AND TRUST

The Sea of Galilee is one of the most vivid "shared places" in the Gospels, a meeting point of water, land, weather, boats, fish, and the daily work of locals. Along its shores, Jesus calls his first disciples, many of whom are fishermen whose lives are intertwined with the lake's rhythms (Matt. 4:18–22; Mk. 1:16–20). Their nets, boats, and the fish they catch are not just props; they are part of the world Jesus enters, transforming an ordinary shoreline into a place of calling and new beginnings (Lk. 5:1–11).

At the water's edge, Jesus teaches from a boat so the crowd can hear him, using the waters and land to communicate truth (Lk. 5:3). From the GHAB perspective, the Sea of Galilee becomes a kind of outdoor sanctuary where human work, nonhuman creatures, and the incarnate Word are connected. Fish fill the nets beyond expectation (Lk. 5:6–7; Jn. 21:5–6), not just as a miracle of provision but as a symbol that creation itself can share in God's generosity.

The lake is also a place where fear and trust are tested. When a storm occurs, and the waves threaten to swamp the boat, the disciples panic while Jesus sleeps (Matt. 8:23–27; Mk. 4:35–41; Lk. 8:22–25). The wind and the sea, which in Israel's imagination often symbolize chaos and danger, respond to his rebuke: "Quiet! Be still!" (Mk. 4:39). At that moment, the Sea of Galilee becomes a classroom where the disciples learn that the One sharing their boat is also Lord over wind, waves, and all creaturely life.

After the resurrection, Jesus returns to the lakeshore to meet his disciples once more (Jn. 21:1–14). There, around a charcoal fire with fish and bread, the Sea of Galilee becomes a place of forgiveness and recommissioning, especially for Peter (Jn. 21:15–19). The beachside meal, shared with the One who is both host and food, hints that God's future with creation will not erase our material world but renew it. In that light, every lake, river, or pasture where we work alongside animals can become, like Galilee, a place of calling and restored fellowship.

THE GARDENS

The gardens are woven throughout Scripture like a scarlet ribbon. From the Garden of Eden (Gen. 2–3) to Jesus' anguish in the Garden of Gethsemane, and even to Jesus being mistaken for a gardener at the empty tomb (Jn. 18:1; 20:15), God repeatedly chooses gardens as places where creation, human life, and God's Spirit come together and are revealed. Gethsemane shows us that redemption happens not in a vague spiritual realm but at a specific place, a garden on the edge of the city, where Jesus struggles with the Father's will amid the world he came to save (Matt. 26:36–46; Mk. 14:32–42; Lk. 22:39–46; cf. Jn. 18:1). This world includes the disciples sleeping nearby and a broader creation that groans in anticipation (Rom. 8:18–23). When read in the context of Eden (Gen. 2–3) and Paul's contrast of the "last Adam" (1 Cor. 15:45–49), Gethsemane becomes a second garden of decision: Christ's obedience begins to repair the fracture of the first garden (Gen. 3). Even when animals are not named, the GHAB is still present here because God's reconciling work touches the entire created world in which Jesus prays, bleeds, is buried, and rises.

THE CROSS: A PLACE OF SACRIFICE AND REDEMPTION

The Cross is the central symbol of suffering, sacrifice, and redemption in the Christian story. On that hill outside the city, Jesus bears the world's brokenness, including the wounds of all creation, and offers himself in love (Heb. 13:12–13; Col. 1:19–20). The Cross itself, the ground on which it stands, and the crowd gathered around it form a fully embodied, creaturely scene.

Though the Cross meets us intimately and is rooted in a real body and a real place, it is also universally efficacious; it accomplishes what God intends. Therefore, the Cross secures cosmic reconciliation for "all things, whether on earth or in heaven" (Col. 1:19–20). God's redeeming work is not far-removed; it is rooted in a real body, in a real place, for the sake of the entire world God has made. The Cross symbolizes the moment when the GHAB (God, humans, and the wider creation) are carried through death and toward renewal. Jesus lived the *missio Dei* in its most costly form (Jn. 1:29; Matt. 21:1–7; Col. 1:19–20).

THE EMPTY TOMB: A PLACE OF NEW CREATION AND HOPE

The empty tomb is a place of transformation, surprise, and new beginnings. In this garden-like setting (Jn. 19:41; 20:1, 11–16), the boundaries of death and despair are broken by Jesus' resurrected life. The sense of place is one of awe, hope, and possibility, a sign that God's promise extends not only to human souls but to "all creation groaning" for renewal (Rom. 8:22–23). The empty tomb becomes a site of encounter with the risen Christ and a preview of the new creation in which all things are made new (1 Cor. 15:20–23; cf. Rev. 21:5). For all creation, this means that the future of animals, ecosystems, and humans depends on Christ's resurrected life (Col. 1:18–20).

THE INCARNATE FOOTPRINTS: PLACES IN JESUS' LIFE

Taken together, these locations in Jesus' life—a manger, the wilderness, the mountains, the temple, the Sea of Galilee, the garden, the Cross, and the tomb—show us that God's mission is rooted in specific places. Each setting reveals how God's presence, human experience, and often animal life intersect in the unfolding of redemption. The nativity draws animals into the first circle of incarnation; the wilderness places Christ among wild creatures; the mountains frame solitude, prayer, and revelation; the temple involves animals, worship, and covenant; Gethsemane situates agony and surrender within a living garden; the Sea of Galilee brings together work, weather, and discipleship into one shared space of calling and trust; the Cross unites earth, body, and history in a single act of costly love; and the empty tomb opens a future of new creation for all that God has made. These are not just holy backdrops to Jesus' story; they are active participants in the *missio Dei* and key windows into the GHAB.

As you think about places in Jesus' life, like the manger, the wilderness, the Sea of Galilee, you may begin to notice *actual* places in your own story: places of work, walking down the sidewalk, parking lots, or dog parks. These, too, can become sites where the GHAB is lived.

THE MEANING OF HOME: HOW PLACES BECOME SACRED THROUGH BELONGING

If God works through burning bushes, arks, temples, stables, and gardens, it should not surprise us that he also works through kitchens, barns, shelters, and backyards. We experience this most intimately in the places we call "home."

Places are gained and lost; they are socially, virtually, and relationally constructed. A place can feel like "home" at a specific moment when time, space, and experience come together to create a sense of belonging. This feeling of home comes when a place becomes meaningful to us through the events, relationships, or emotions associated with it. In other words, it is the combination of time, location, and personal experience that turns a simple spot into a place we call "home." This reflects the saying, "Home is where you are."

It is crucial to remember that God is not simply an afterthought in this process. God's reconciling Spirit is everywhere, uniting all creation and inviting us into relationship, restoration, and wholeness. When we recognize our homes and familiar places as shared sites where God, humans, and animals meet, we begin to see how ordinary spaces become sacred through belonging and love.

BRIDGING THE SACRED AND THE EVERYDAY: GRAVES, DONKEYS, AND JUSTICE

If places and animals can serve as living markers of God's presence, then even what we might call the "leftovers" of history, like bones, graves, and work animals, all have theological meaning.

The graves of sacrificed animals also serve as placeholders, providing archaeological and historical insight into the lives, beliefs, and cultures of ancient peoples. Animal remains are like placeholders in history, enabling archaeologists to continue telling human–animal stories. Over the past several decades, archaeological research on animal burials and sacrifice has shed new light on the roles animals played in ancient worship and daily life.[6]

Through these research efforts, we find that, in most cases, the wealthy could afford to purchase a large sacrificial animal at market prices. In contrast, a poor person could sacrifice only animals from their own farm or buy a seemingly less significant animal. In other words, even at the altar, social and economic divisions were on display. These graves and remains, as historical placeholders, keep a space open in our memory and imagination for the economic realities and animal lives bound up in ancient worship.

In atonement theology, Jesus' death on the Cross is understood as the climactic temple sacrifice, which is why John calls him "the Lamb of God, who takes away the sin of the world" (Jn. 1:29, 36). In Jesus, God provides a single, sufficient offering that is not limited by class, status, or the size of one's flock (or bank account); the rich and the poor alike depend on the same Lamb.

So, Jesus enters Jerusalem on a young donkey to assert his identity as a different kind of King and to fulfill prophecy (Matt. 21:1–4; Zech. 9:9). He could have entered the city on foot or ridden a warhorse, but instead chose an animal commonly used as a beast of burden, which is a deeply symbolic choice. According to Jewish law, the donkey was considered unclean and required redemption (Exod. 13:13).[7] Yet farmers in both the ancient world and today value its usefulness because it can carry heavy loads. Seen this way, the animal becomes a living metaphor: the humble, unclean creature that transports the Holy One into the city where he will bear the world's sin.

The contrast is intentional: the King chooses to ride an

animal that reflects our own unclean condition. It is not a contradiction but a living picture of the gospel, where those who are humble and considered unclean are raised up and carried by Christ's grace.

In this Christic sign or placeholder, the lamb and the donkey stand together as living markers of atonement, signs that God's atoning work embraces both rich and poor and reaches all the way down into the life of the animals and the land that have carried our burdens for so long.[8] This Christologically rich scene and historical placeholder evokes an image of the donkey (unclean) and the Lamb of God (clean) entering the world's altar, Jerusalem, together, another powerful image of the GHAB.

These patterns reveal that the GHAB has prophetic roots and that God has always worked through animals and places to tell his story. They also remind us that any theology of place must be attentive to social and economic divisions, to which animals and landscapes silently bear witness.

MISSIONAL THEOLOGY IN PRACTICE

If Scripture's places and Jesus' own footprints show us how God works in real places, then our call is to live out a missional theology that takes our own shared places seriously; for example, our houses, yards, job sites, and schoolyards.

I have talked to many pet owners about the GHAB, and they intuitively recognize both the relationship and the spiritual significance it holds, regardless of their religious beliefs. Followers of Christ have a deep desire for people to be healed and find comfort. I imagine we also want people to be kinder to one another and to experience true peace in their lives and communities. We know God is the source of all love, peace, and unity.

Each Christian, drawing on their unique mental, physical, emotional, and spiritual resources and abilities, is called to show love and generosity to others, including local neighbors and those far away. In today's globalized world, loving our neighbor on the other side of the planet does not always require travel or international missionary work (though those are wonderful); it often requires intentional choices in our daily lives about what we eat, wear, and do.

In conversations with our customers, I'm often struck by how naturally they speak about the depth and meaning of their relationships with their dogs. They may not use the language of the GHAB, but they sense that something more than "pet ownership" is happening. For me, those conversations are not projects or strategies; they are gifts, glimpses into how deeply people care and how God may already be at work in their lives through the animals they love.

EVERYDAY ENCOUNTERS: LIVING OUT MISSIONAL THEOLOGY

I think of missional theology as a living stream (Jn. 7:38) that flows into unknown regions of the world around us. Some will only dip their toe in; others will drink deeply (Jn. 4:14). Richard Rohr writes:

> *"We all breathe the same air and drink the same water. There are no Jewish, Christian, or Muslim versions of these universal elements. All water is 'Holy water' even before the benefit of a priest's waved hand. It is always and everywhere two parts hydrogen and one part oxygen, and voilà—we have the absolute miracle of liquid water, absolutely necessary for all that lives."*[9]

Maybe you have already tasted the living water, and your intention has allowed it to change your life, as it did for me. Or perhaps you are standing at the shore, deciding whether to step in. If we extend the metaphor, we can imagine the stream flowing over hills and through valleys in some places, and in others, running through big cities where concrete now replaces the dirt banks.

The stream represents God's mission and our choice to participate in it, but its form depends on one's personal context. My ministry might look very different from yours, whether you are in your neighborhood, your workplace, or simply sharing God's love in everyday moments. But the living water itself never changes. It has been the same for thousands of years and always will be. Our task is to share everything God has given us, whether someone is already swimming in the depths, curious about what the water feels like, or hesitant even to come close.

In my cultural context, I try to help people wherever I am: when someone drops off or picks up their dog at our home, where we offer boarding, or during unexpected encounters while I'm out shopping or doing everyday tasks. Sometimes that means a quick word of spiritual insight or a prayer offered in passing, simple gestures that still carry a touch of God's love. I choose, and keep choosing, to trust Jesus, and I long for my life to be a living expression of God's love. Like all followers of Jesus, I need to be intentional about sharing what I have learned in the places where I live and work. When we open our homes and hearts, sharing our stories, struggles, and joys in Jesus' name, we participate in God's mission. It is about intentionally living out our faith in everyday moments and sharing Christ's hope with the world around us.

Likewise, the natural world and its creatures often witness to more profound spiritual truths: a squirrel's relentless pursuit of acorns teaches us the value of persistence; a cat's disapproving stare reminds us to mind our own business. If we can learn patience from waiting for a turtle to decide to cross the road, perhaps we are on the right path. Just as we recognize the importance of caring for the vulnerable, whether a fragile rabbit or a fellow human, our faith calls us to extend love and protection beyond ourselves. The seasonal cycle of new life and renewal serves as a poignant reminder of the divine presence in all living things, urging us to embody the compassion and stewardship that reflect God's own love for creation.

When we see our neighborhoods, churches, barns, and back roads as places where God, humans, and animals meet, we start to realize that most places can be shared. Shared places become a part of creation where the GHAB unfolds, and God's mission is lived out.

QUESTIONS FOR REFLECTION AND PRACTICE

- As you reflect on the places in Jesus' life, what specific locations from your own story come to mind where God, humans, and animals have met? How might you start to see those places as active participants in God's mission rather than just extras in a scene?
- This week, choose *one* ordinary place that you visit often (such as a kitchen, cafe, sidewalk, office, or dog park) and spend a few extra minutes there in prayerful awareness. What shifts when you ask, "How is God already at work here, and how are the animals and people sharing this place part of that work?"

NOTES

1. Gordon J. Wenham, *Genesis 1–15*, Word Biblical Commentary 1 (Waco, TX: Word Books, 1987), 4–5, 180–81; Walter Brueggemann, *Genesis*, Interpretation (Atlanta: John Knox Press, 1982), 29–30, 79–80.
2. See also Gerhard von Rad, *Genesis: A Commentary*, rev. ed., Old Testament Library (Philadelphia: Westminster, 1972), 49–51, 113–18.
3. On the traditional inclusion of animals at the manger and its link to Isa. 1:3, see studies of how the nativity story has been depicted in Christian art and worship (reception history). Luke does not explicitly name animals; the church has imagined them as present to depict creation's participation in the Incarnation. I follow this traditional imagery theologically rather than as a claim about Luke's historical detail.
4. For differing interpretations of Mark 1:13 ("with the wild animals"), see, e.g., Ched Myers, *Binding the Strong Man: A Political Reading of Mark's Story of Jesus* (Maryknoll, NY: Orbis Books, 1988), and Joel Marcus, *Mark 1–8: A New Translation with Introduction and Commentary*, Anchor Yale Bible 27 (New Haven, CT: Yale University Press, 2000). My reading emphasizes the Son's solidarity with creation. Although, some scholars read the "wild animals" as part of the danger of the wilderness (e.g., Myers; Marcus), while others see here an early sign of creation's reconciliation with the Messiah; see, for example, Richard Bauckham, *Jesus and the Wild Animals (Mk. 1:13): A Christological Image for an Ecological Age*, in *Jesus and the God of Israel* (Grand Rapids: Eerdmans, 2008). I adopt the latter emphasis as an early glimpse of the GHAB.
5. G. K. Beale, *The Temple and the Church's Mission: A Biblical Theology of the Dwelling Place of God*, New Studies in Biblical Theology 17 (Downers Grove, IL: InterVarsity Press, 2004), 29–80.
6. On animal sacrifice, burials, and social stratification in the

ancient world, see, for example, Kenneth C. Way, *Donkeys in the Biblical World: Ceremony and Symbol* (Winona Lake, IN: Eisenbrauns, 2011), 18–19.

7. George P. van Kooten, "Exodus 13:13a: The Donkey and the Lamb," *Christian Library*, accessed May 7, 2022, *https://www.christianstudylibrary.org/article/exodus-1313a-donkey-and-lamb.*

8. For a Christological reading of animal imagery and atonement, see Jn. 1:29, 36; Exod. 13:13; and the broader canonical use of lamb and donkey as symbolic creatures within Israel's sacrificial and social life.

9. Richard Rohr, *The Universal Christ: How a Forgotten Reality Can Change Everything We See, Hope For, and Believe* (New York: Convergent, 2019), 56.

5

A SHARED EXPERIENCE

In the previous chapter, I focused on *where* God, humans, and animals meet, places where they are active participants in God's mission. Now, I'm moving from biblical and theological foundations to practical theology. This chapter turns to what happens *within* those places, the *shared experiences* and relationships through which the GHAB becomes real.

In 2023, Winston and I became a therapy animal team with Pet Partners, a trained human-animal pair certified to visit people in professional settings. This national non-profit is dedicated to evaluating and certifying human-animal teams to visit specialized settings, like hospitals. Pet Partner is dedicated to enhancing health and happiness through the power of the HAB (Human-Animal Bond). While Pet Partners focuses on the HAB, I see Winston's work within the broader GHAB framework, where healing interactions are lived moments in which God, humans, and an animal share in God's ongoing mission.

I witnessed this clearly during a visit to a care facility shortly after one of their residents died unexpectedly. He had been there regularly for care and social interaction, and his sudden absence left the staff and other residents grieving. Amid that heaviness, the director invited us to visit. That week, Winston became the first donkey ever to walk into their group room.

We entered slowly, and Winston went from person to person, visiting each resident individually. As he did, his presence brought smiles and laughter to faces that had been weighed down by loss. I found myself explaining that donkeys are often called *beasts of burden*, and in a symbolic way, animals like Winston can help us *name and share* our troubles when we place our hands on them. In that moment, I felt less like a visitor and more like a pastor, inviting the room into a shared spiritual practice of placing our grief on this humble creature and trusting that the Lord would receive that touch as prayer. As residents stroked his coat and rested their hands on his back, it felt as though some of the weight in the room was being shared. It was as if Winston were holding a piece of their sorrow, and God was meeting them there.

MYSTICISM AS AN ANTIDOTE TO OBJECTIFICATION

Animals are more than simple objects serving practical purposes. When we see other creatures, whether animals or humans, as existing solely for our benefit, we miss who they really are. The trees are for the birds, the fields for the cows to graze, and the oceans for the fish to swim in. In their work on the church and creation, theologians John Mark Hicks, Bobby Valentine, and Mark Wilson remind us of our role in creation: "We fulfill our role as God's priests by enabling creation to become what God created it to be."[1]

Most of us, though, spend a lot of time removed from the natural world. We build fences, walls, and schedules that keep us indoors and online, creating artificial boundaries. Learning to recognize God's eternal attributes in the world around us, to sit with what they mean, and to receive them as gifts is one way of naming mystical theology. When we move beyond our self-made separations and rediscover a sense of kinship with the natural world, ordinary moments can become sacred moments. It is this deep, attentive presence with God, often called a mystical experience, that transforms ordinary encounters with creation into moments of real connection. It would be helpful to point out that mystical attentiveness is not an escape from the world but a way of joining God's mission more deeply, because it trains us to see and honor the creatures and places through which God is already at work.

For example, when I take a walk with my friend, a Walker Coonhound named Maisy, I try to choose a path that suits her nature: beneath the canopy of trees, along a dirt trail, or across an open field. I sometimes joke that "I'm meeting the need of the breed," but underneath the joke is something more serious. It is an act of shared joy and mindful presence. Maisy's hunting instincts pull her into the woods, where she can follow the scents of animals that foraged overnight, fully awake to the world God made.

As we walk, I mentally practice *lectio terra*, a discipline similar to *lectio divina*, but focused on reading the landscape as God's living text. Each rustle in the underbrush and each bird call nudges me closer to prayer.

Walking with Maisy seems to draw me into an engagement with the world around us. Our walk turns into a kind of ecological discipleship, dog-led, of course. When I frame it as a prayerful practice, I'm more likely to notice the Holy in the sensory details: the smell of damp earth and the texture of leaves underfoot. My connection to the earth deepens, and then I find myself hoping that others might be moved to notice their own dog walks or backyard moments in a similar way.

Of course, Maisy would happily walk with me anywhere, even on hot pavement and city sidewalks, simply because we are together. But what brings her the greatest joy is hunting in the fields as she was made to do: nose to the ground, wind in her ears, surrounded by the subtle music and scent of the woods. Choosing to walk with her this way reminds me that we, too, are meant to be open and pay attention to the Spirit's qualities, freedom, play, and life, as they are expressed in creation.

Mysticism, then, is not always found in visions or mountaintop experiences; it also resides in these very ordinary moments. It appears when we approach the world with openness and share in another's happiness. In honoring Maisy's true nature, I'm also drawn back into my own. Her joy calls me to notice that the line between human and animal, and between what we call sacred and ordinary, is much more porous than we often imagine.

BEING WITH: THE GIFT OF PRESENCE

One of the deepest spiritual lessons my animals have taught me is the value of simple, attentive presence. If God had a love language, I suspect it would be presence.

Some of my happiest moments are the ordinary ones with dogs, mine and other people's. Twig, Aspen, and Willow come to the porch with me almost every time I step outside, not because I have a plan, but because being together is enough. There's always a little rush at first: eager tail-wagging, playful wet-nose nudges, a burst of energy as they find a place to rest; then we settle.

We sit side by side and listen to the mockingbirds and killdeer, taking in the breeze. The dogs aren't trying to accomplish anything; they simply want to be near me. Dogs naturally crave the company of their friends, and the way they rest in our presence can remind us of God's own desire to be with us.

Scripture affirms this. Genesis 1:1–2 says, "In the beginning God created the heavens and the earth…and the Spirit of God was hovering over the waters." God's presence is not distant but intimately involved in creation. Psalm 19:1 echoes this: "The heavens declare the glory of God; the skies proclaim the work of his hands." Both passages describe a God who is actively involved in creation, not detached.

The challenge is for us to recognize and respond to this presence. You might look at your dog and say aloud, "Thank you, Lord, for giving me this furry companion. He's the best listener." Or you may look at your sick dog and simply notice your heart swell, warm and full, without needing to speak. The provisions themselves, and the way your heart feels as if it is exploding with emotion, are gifts from God and signs that the Spirit is with you.

While we often think about how humans respond to God, it's also interesting to consider how a dog might react to God's presence. A dog's natural senses, such as being alert, receptive, or joyful, can show us what it means to live in the presence of the Creator. When a dog lifts its nose to the wind (a behavior called "winding"), wags its tail, and its eyes sparkle with curiosity, it seems instinctively connected to the goodness of creation. Through their uninhibited trust and loyalty, a dog's actions can appear to reflect a kind of worship: a wholehearted, physical response to the gift of life.

When my dogs rest at my feet, relaxed and at peace, I can almost see in them a model for my own spiritual posture: trusting, grateful, and open to the love that surrounds me. Their simple, genuine response to the world encourages us to do the same: to notice, to be present, and to rest in the awareness that God is always near.

SEEING: THE GIFT OF RECOGNITION

There is a gray-and-white stray cat that has learned to watch for the barn door to crack open so our outdoor cat, Myshka, can go in and out. When the door is ajar, the stray cat slips inside, eats from Myshka's kibble, and then dashes back across the road to our neighbor's house.

Since our driveway runs beside the barn, I sometimes see this cat watching from the field when I get out of the car. Many times, I have noticed and simply gone about my business. One evening, though, as I walked out to close the barn, I saw the cat again and decided to do something different. I left a small pile of kibble on the step next to the barn door, as if to say, "I see you, and I care." It was only a small gesture, and it did not erase all the times I had looked away, but it reminded me how powerful a single act of recognition can be.

I realize how powerful a simple acknowledgment can be, even in the smallest relationships. If I walk past my cat, Myshka, day after day without looking at her or pausing to connect, she seems to shrink back, as if unnoticed. When I slow down enough to say hello or give her a little pat on the head, I'm reminded that she, too, is someone in my daily world, a small but real partner in the bond God has given us. In a sense, the act of seeing, whether human or animal, trains my mind and changes my actions to honor the presence and worth of those who share my life.

Alexandra Horowitz, in *Inside of a Dog*, emphasizes this same dynamic from a different angle: much of a dog's well-being depends on being truly seen and understood by their human companions.[2] Many people even admit to greeting their dogs before their spouses when they come home. While some might criticize this, it reflects a deeper truth that runs through every meaningful relationship, human and animal alike: at the core lies a longing to be recognized and cherished.

PRACTICING PRESENCE AND SEEING

As you reflect on your own life, consider these questions of presence and seeing:

- » When have you experienced the joy of simply being with God or another creature?
- » Are there moments when you think you may have overlooked God's presence, whether in creation, in others, or in yourself? (Hindsight is powerful for seeing where God was in your life.)
- » Whom do you honestly see each day, and who might be longing to be seen by you?

Let the lessons learned from God's creatures draw you into a deeper practice of presence and a more attentive way of seeing the world. In doing so, you may find yourself encountering God in new, unexpected places, even right beside you on the porch or in your pet's eyes.

SACRED BONDS: THE HOLY FOUNDATION IN HUMAN-ANIMAL STORIES

It is difficult to deny the evidence of God in the world. People may witness an indescribable sunset or a massive wall cloud bending toward the earth and yet choose to reject or rename these wonders as having origins other than God. However, Romans 1:20 affirms, "For since the creation of the world God's invisible qualities—his eternal power and divine nature—have been clearly seen, being understood from what has been made, so that people are without excuse."

This truth emerges not only in Scripture but also in the stories we cherish, narratives that reveal deep connections between humans and animals. In *Where the Red Fern Grows*, a boy's devotion to his dogs and their costly loyalty to him expose how love can be both fiercely joyful and heartbreakingly sacrificial. In *The Call of the Wild* and *White Fang*, Jack London shows animals moving between wildness and companionship, revealing how a creature can belong to and be transformed by a human friend. And in Pamela Turner's retelling of *Hachikō: The True Story of a Loyal Dog*, a dog's unshakable daily vigil for his deceased owner becomes a living icon of faithfulness. These stories are tearjerkers because they touch the places in us that know love is real, costly, and enduring; they echo the Holy bond at the heart of the GHAB, where God's own faithful love is mirrored in the lives of animals who stay, suffer, and remain with us.

A DOG'S UTOPIA: OUR HOME AS SHARED SPACE

Before describing the practices that shape A Dog's Utopia, it may be helpful to explain what it is. A Dog's Utopia is not a separate facility or storefront; it is our home. It is the place where we live, welcome dogs into our daily rhythms, and open our doors to the people who love them. On the surface, it might look like an ordinary house with a fenced yard, toys scattered across the grass, water bowls refreshed throughout the day, and dogs napping in sunlit corners. For the dogs, it is a safe, practical, and familiar arrangement, but for us it has become something more: a shared space where the GHAB is lived out in ordinary ways.

From the beginning, we sensed that this work was not only about providing safe, reliable care, but about honoring each dog as a beloved creature held in God's hands. Over time, we began to notice patterns: anxious dogs settling into peace, lonely people finding connection through simple conversations at drop-off and pick-up, and everyday moments in our kitchen or backyard becoming *thin places,* God's presence felt especially near. In the Celtic Christian tradition, thin places are moments or locations where the veil between heaven and earth feels especially transparent. One afternoon, for example, a client arrived to pick up her dog after a long week of caring for an ill parent. As she knelt to greet her dog, he pressed his head into her chest and simply leaned there, still and breathing deeply. For a moment, the front yard seemed still around us, and it felt as though time had slowed, the grief, the relief, and the comfort all held together in that ordinary embrace. It was a small thing, yet it carried the weight of prayer.

A Dog's Utopia has become one of the primary contexts in which we live the GHAB, a place where our home, our work, and our love for animals are linked together and where we live out these sacred experiences.

What follows, then, are not undefined principles but practices we are still learning to embody in this particular place. These principles of missional living have grown out of our experience at A Dog's Utopia. Yet, they can be adapted to many other homes and settings where people, animals, and God's Spirit meet.

A DOG'S UTOPIA: PRINCIPLES OF MISSIONAL LIVING

Building on this understanding of interconnectedness and shared vocation, our practices at A Dog's Utopia aim to embody these principles in daily life.

Prayerful Presence: We include our customers and their dogs in our prayers, and when someone is hurting, we let them know we are praying and, if they wish, offer prayer.

Stewardship: We treat every animal entrusted to us with respect and compassion as we shepherd them. I use the word shepherd intentionally: we are not merely managing dogs as a service, but caring for them as living beings entrusted to us for a season. Like a shepherd who understands the needs and limits of each sheep, we pay attention to each dog's temperament, fears, and joys, protecting them from harm and helping them feel safe and seen while they are with us. Our care does not end at the gate; we also check on them after they return home, trusting that the GHAB continues beyond our front door.

Community: We aim to create a place where the bonds between people, animals, and God are celebrated, staying attentive and open to those moments when God's presence feels especially close, the "thin places," where the sacred and ordinary meet.

Storytelling: We encourage sharing experiences that showcase God's goodness in creation, help others see their lives as part of a larger, sacred story, and demonstrate how they can include their dogs in these stories. One simple way we do this is through the Rover platform, which works like our online administrative assistant: we send daily updates, pictures, and short videos so owners can see how their dogs are doing and remember that their own lives, and their animals' lives, are part of God's ongoing story.

By embracing these principles, we pray that our work becomes a deliberate act of glorifying God, reminding ourselves and those we serve that living a Christ-centered life means caring deeply for all of God's creation. Through prayer, stewardship, community, and storytelling, we engage in the ongoing work of partnering with God within the GHAB.

A GOD–HUMAN–ANIMAL PRAYER

This is the prayer my spouse and I share with the diverse clients of A Dog's Utopia who entrust their beloved dogs to us. By naming God's presence in these relationships and interceding for both humans and animals, we understand this shared prayer as our *intentional* participation in the *missio Dei*.

We hope that, regardless of their spiritual beliefs or backgrounds, our clients will discern the depth of our love and concern for their dogs. Our care is grounded in the love of God, and we understand this work as participation in His mission and as an expression of our intentional presence to those whom God places in our path.

OUR GOD-HUMAN-ANIMAL PRAYER FOR YOU

Lord, may You continue to enlighten us
all to the mysteries of creation,
namely, the dogs in our care.
We give thanks.
Our greatest gift is to partner with you, Lord,
and ourcustomers, to care for their dogs
in our humble home.
We give thanks.
You bestow blessings that manifest in a full circle
to the dogs,customers, us, and back to you.
We give thanks.
The relationships we have with the dogs
elicit our spiritual imaginations, which help us
to re-imagine the creative ways you reach us.
We give thanks.
We welcome the experiences you reveal through
every dog's divine micro-expressions of faith,
hope, and love.
We give thanks.
We commit to co-labor with you to share
in creation's diverse dog breeds, ages,
personality types, and playfulness.
We give thanks.
May your peace be upon all our customers
and their dogs.
In Christ's name we pray,
Amen.

EXPLANATION OF PRAYER

This prayer rests on two key Scriptures. First, Colossians 1:16: "For in him all things were created: things in heaven and on earth, visible and invisible... all things have been created through him and for him." Christ is both the origin and the goal of all creation. Everything, including animals and the natural world, finds its true purpose and worth in him.

Second, John 20:21 highlights Jesus' mission: "Peace be with you! As the Father has sent me, I am sending you." Jesus offers peace and then sends his followers to continue his reconciling work. This mission extends to all God has made. Just as Christ was sent to bring healing to a broken world, we are sent to join in God's ongoing mission.

Together, these passages emphasize the sacredness of all creation and the calling of Christ's followers to act as stewards and ambassadors of God's peace, mirroring Christ's love to every creature and place.

The refrain "We give thanks" echoes a recurring biblical theme: "Give thanks to the Lord, for he is good; his love endures forever" (1 Chron. 16:34; Ps. 107:1; 118:1). Gratitude keeps us rooted in God's unchanging goodness as we engage in this work.

"May God continue to enlighten us all to the mysteries of creation, namely the dogs in our care," urges us to attend to how God's character is reflected in the animals we serve. John 14:10–11 reminds us that Jesus' actions express his unity with the Father; in caring for animals, we seek to act out of that same shared life.

"Our greatest gift is partnering with you, Lord, and our customers to care for the dogs in our humble home." This partnership reflects the *perichoretic* dance of the Trinity, in which every movement is coordinated in love. Psalm 139:7–10 affirms that God's presence surrounds us wherever we go, and John 17:21 highlights that we are called into a unity that reflects the mutual indwelling of Father and Son. Our relationships with customers and animals are meant to participate in that unity and love.

"You bestow blessings that manifest in a full circle to the dogs, customers, us, and back to you." James 1:17 says, "Every good and perfect gift is from above... who does not change like shifting shadows." God's gifts are meant to circulate outward in service and return in praise. When we bless people and animals with kindness and care, we join a cycle of blessing that points toward the renewal and restoration promised in Romans 8.

"The relationships we have with the dogs elicit our spiritual imaginations, which help us re-imagine the creative ways you reach us." Our imaginations must be tuned to God's work, much like a shepherd is alert to the flock. We have noticed divine "micro-expressions" of faith, hope, and love—owners trusting us, hoping their dogs will thrive, and dogs greeting them with joy. 1 Corinthians 13:13 reminds us that "these three remain: faith, hope, and love. But the greatest of these is love."

In this sacred dance, many of our canine companions' behaviors reflect the Spirit moving within creation, echoing the divine breath that sustains life. John 1:14 proclaims, "The Word became flesh and made his dwelling among us... full of grace and truth." Christ, the Good Shepherd, embodies God's love in tangible form, inviting us to glimpse his glory in everyday moments. Ephesians 3:20 tells us that God is able "to do immeasurably more than all we ask or imagine," and Genesis 1:31 affirms that "God saw all that he had made, and it was very good." Our imaginations, stirred by the loving presence of animals, become a sacred lens through which we perceive God's ongoing revelation and the beauty of his creation.

"We commit to co-labor with you to share in creation's diverse dog breeds, ages, personality types, and playfulness." Psalm 104:24 rejoices, "How many are your works, Lord! In wisdom you made them all; the earth is full of your creatures." John 20:21 reminds us again that we are sent ones, called to bring Christ's peace into all our relationships, including those with animals.

"May your peace be upon all our customers and their dogs." Matthew 10:29–31 assures us that not even a sparrow falls outside the Father's care. Our animals and we are included in that same attentive love.

"In Christ's name we pray, Amen." Romans 8:38–39 declares that nothing in all creation can separate us from the love of God in Christ. Ending our prayer in Christ's name affirms our confidence in that unbreakable love.

The Christian tradition has a word for the inner life of divine love: *perichoresis*, the mutual indwelling and vibrant relationship of Father, Son, and Spirit—a harmonious dance that reaches outward, inviting all creation into its embrace. When we pray in Christ's name and say "amen," we affirm our place in that relationship and trust in God's faithfulness. 2 Corinthians 1:20 reminds us that all of God's promises are "Yes" in Christ, and that our "Amen" is spoken to the glory of God.

Seen together, these are moments of connection, as with Winston, Maisy, Myshka, a stray cat, or the guest dogs at A Dog's Utopia; they represent a chain. Each story is a single link, complete in itself yet meant to connect to the next. Over time, these God–human–animal encounters reveal a pattern: a living chain of grace that runs through our days, reminding us that the GHAB is not an isolated experience but an ongoing, unbreakable connection held together by God.

QUESTIONS FOR REFLECTION AND PRACTICE

» Think back over this chapter's stories with Winston, Maisy, Twig, Aspen, and Willow, the stray cat at the barn, and the experiences at A Dog's Utopia. Which scene feels closest to something in your own life? How might that memory be a place where God, you, and an animal shared a moment of healing, comfort, or joy?

» This week, choose one simple practice of "being with" or "seeing" more attentively as you are sitting on the porch with a dog, noticing a stray, greeting an animal in your neighborhood, or including a pet in a moment of prayer. What happens when you intentionally treat that shared experience as part of the GHAB and as a small participation in the *missio Dei*?

NOTES

1. John Mark Hicks, Bobby Valentine, and Mark Wilson, *A Gathered People: Revisioning the Assembly as Transforming Encounter* (Abilene, TX: Leafwood Publishers, 2007), 179.
2. Alexandra Horowitz, *Inside of a Dog: What Dogs See, Smell, and Know* (New York: Scribner, 2010), 250-280.

6

A SHARED SPIRIT

CONDUIT AND SOURCE

On our farm, a hidden system of pipes and casing draws water from deep underground to our kitchen tap. That well has become my clearest picture of what a conduit is. The water level sits roughly eighty feet below, where the unseen water supply finally emerges. From there, a pipe carries that deep, hidden water to our house, where a filtration system removes impurities before the water reaches our taps. I do not see any of this, but its purpose is clear: to deliver fresh, life-giving water where it is needed, while protecting it along the way.

This particular well did not come easily. The former owners drilled twice and came up dry both times. On the third attempt, the well company brought in a man with an old skill sometimes called "witching" or dowsing. A neighbor remembers watching him walk the land in a big straw hat, holding two forked sticks that, he said, would cross when he passed over water. However, we were told that day, the third spot he marked is the well that now supplies our house, animals, and fields.

That story humbles me. It reminds me that the water we drink, the buckets we fill in the barn, and the tap I turn on without thinking are not guaranteed. They depend on a hidden aquifer, on the work and discernment of people who came before us, and ultimately on God's silent provision beneath our feet.

Over time, I have come to see the Triune God as the

ultimate source in my life. Just as a pipe channels water from the well to my home and a filtration system purifies it, the Father is the deep source; Christ is the conduit who brings grace and salvation from God's heart into my life; and the Holy Spirit is the living stream of that grace, continually sustaining, cleansing, and renewing me day by day. The Spirit cleanses, protects, maintains, and nourishes in ways I may not always see but rely on. Like the constant flow of water through my home, the Spirit is always present.

PAUSE AND REMEMBER

The Holy Spirit carries God's grace from depths we cannot see into the most minor details of our lives, moving through every moment like water through a house, sustaining and cleansing. For a moment, consider opening new "conduits" for that grace this week through intentional prayer, a shared meal, or a simple act of service in your community.

JESUS AS CONDUIT OF THE SPIRIT

Jesus' role as a conduit is shown clearly when he gives the Holy Spirit to his disciples in John 20:19–23. On the evening of the first day of the week, as the disciples gathered behind locked doors out of fear, Jesus appeared among them and said, "Peace be with you!" After showing them his hands and side, he repeated, "Peace be with you! As the Father has sent me, I am sending you." Then he breathed on them and said, "Receive the Holy Spirit. If you forgive anyone's sins, their sins are forgiven; if you do not forgive them, they are not forgiven."

In this sacred moment, Jesus acts as the Holy conduit

through whom the Father's purposes flow, connecting heaven and earth and uniting the divine and human in one sending. Through his life, death, and resurrection, the bond between God and creation, including humanity and the animal Kingdom, is carried through death toward renewal. By his sacrifice and by the power of the Spirit, we are upheld, renewed, and invited into the ongoing flow of God's love and restoration.

SPIRIT, CREATION, AND REDEMPTION

The biblical words for Spirit—Hebrew *ruakh* and Greek *pneuma*—refer to God's own breath, wind, and life-giving presence that moves through the world. In 2 Timothy 3:16, Scripture itself is called *theopneustos*, a Greek term meaning "God-breathed," serving as a reminder that the same divine breath that animates creation also inspires the written testimony that guides our understanding. Together, they bear witness to a God whose Spirit energizes and sustains all living beings, human and non-human alike. If that same Spirit truly fills and renews creation, then redemption cannot be limited to the inner life of individual believers; it must also be environmental (affecting land, water, and nonhuman creatures), cultural (shaping our habits, systems, and stories), and cosmic (embracing the entire created order in Christ). For those of us working with the GHAB, this means the Spirit's work includes healing relationships between people and animals, restoring broken places, and re-patterning our communities' imagination of what faithful stewardship looks like. By paying close attention to how the Spirit moves through the world, we find hope for healing, reconciliation, and growth within the GHAB.

SPIRIT AS THE SHEPHERD

Besides breath, Scripture also describes the Spirit as a guide and shepherd, leading, comforting, and renewing both people and creation. The psalmist declares, "When you send your Spirit, they are created, and you renew the face of the ground" (Ps. 104:30). Renewal is not only inward; it touches the land and the communities that depend on it.

Personal renewal occurs when exhausted people regain strength after a sabbatical, retreat, or season of rest. Environmental renewal, often described through ecotheology, grounds our care for the earth in our understanding of God. It includes restoring wetlands or reviving wildlife, as well as the ways communities rebuild after hardship.

When I first took Winston to visit large groups of children and counseling centers, I wasn't sure how he would cope with the large crowds, tight spaces, and strangers with unpredictable behavior reaching for him. Even though he had already passed the formal behavioral evaluation required for therapy-animal teams, I still felt the weight of responsibility for his safety and the safety of the people we met. Before each visit, I would pause in the barn aisle and pray, "Spirit, guide us. Help me see who needs us today. Help Winston stay calm and safe." As we were inside the building, I watched as the Spirit seemed to lead us, not with an audible voice, but through inward nudges: a patient who kept staring out the window until Winston entered the doorway; a nurse who burst into tears the moment she touched his neck; a child who was too anxious to speak until she started talking to him. Over time, I learned to trust that the same Spirit who renews the face of the ground (Ps. 104:30) was also guiding our steps, protecting Winston from harm, and directing us toward the people who needed that specific kind of comfort. This is the work of a Shepherd.

SPIRIT AS THE REDEEMER

Redemption, like renewal, is broad in scope. Spiritually, people seek forgiveness and transformation after failure: "Repent, then, and turn to God, so that your sins may be wiped out, that times of refreshing may come from the Lord" (Acts 3:19). In literature, flawed characters set out to make things right. In public life, societies pursue redemption when they honestly confront collective wrongs, through truth-telling, reparations, or long-term work for justice after slavery, apartheid, or genocide.

These are not merely human efforts. Wherever genuine restoration of relationships and systems takes place, we see signs of the Spirit at work, pressing toward reconciliation in human hearts and in the broader world.

To see how this redeeming work of the Spirit has been perceived over time, we turn now to Jesus' life as the Christic paradigm and to mystics who bore witness to the Spirit's movement in their own contexts.

THE HISTORICAL JESUS AND THE RESURRECTED CHRIST

Sallie McFague, a leading Christian ecological theologian, insists that "the Christic paradigm must precede the cosmic Christ."[1] The historical Jesus refers to the life, ministry, and incarnation of Jesus, the concrete, historical person who embodies divine love in a particular time and place. The resurrected Christ, by contrast, is the universal, risen Christ who holds all things together: "He is before all things, and in him all things hold together" (Col. 1:17).

McFague's point is crucial: we cannot jump directly into abstract talk of a cosmic Christ without first grounding our faith in Jesus, whose life and sacrificial love reveal God's heart. The incarnation shows that God's care for creation is not just theoretical; it is lived, relational, and specific. The Spirit's work in the world flows from Jesus' life and love, and only then can we accurately speak of the global and cosmic scope of redemption. In this book, I work within that same pattern: the GHAB is not a cosmic idea but a Spirit-given participation in the concrete life and love of Jesus, which then extends outward to include all living things. We see this movement whenever a person, drawn more deeply into Christ's life by the Spirit, begins to care differently for the creatures and places around them, like a farmer who changes how they treat their animals or a veterinarian who prays over a frightened patient.

Therefore, the Spirit's renewal and redemption are not merely abstract spiritual ideas; they produce *tangible* effects on our lives, animals, and the earth. We unforgettably experienced this when we adopted a young Golden Retriever from a family who no longer wanted her. On her first night with us, we were petting her and checking her over when we noticed her breath smelled far worse than it should for a dog her age. Looking into her mouth, we saw a stick lodged tightly between her front teeth. It had been there so long that her gums had begun to grow around it. We knew it would hurt, but with firm pressure, we pulled it free. She flinched, but what followed was relief we could not measure in words. The next day, we took her to the veterinarian for vaccines and a dental cleaning. Afterwards, we also learned that she did not tolerate small dogs well, a need in a home like ours. So, after making sure she had received the care she needed, we returned her to her original family, trusting that, with her pain addressed, she would be easier to live with and more at peace. It was not a perfect ending or a storybook adoption. However, it *still* offered a glimpse of the Spirit's renewing work: hidden suffering was brought to light, real pain was addressed, and both a dog and a family were given a better chance to thrive.

WAYS THE ANCIENT MYSTICS EXPERIENCED THE SPIRIT

It may be illuminating to read from the ancient mystics to realize the history we share. These mystics do not merely offer theological abstractions about the Spirit, but witness to a lived reality. Their testimonies demonstrate that the Spirit's work is not confined to the human soul; it is a spiritual force that encompasses humans, animals, and all living things within a single divine breath, creating a sacred bond. This relevance is vital for future work in creating communities that are not only spiritually alive but also ecologically aware.

By engaging with several of the ancient mystics, we see that the Spirit's presence is experienced in various ways: as life-giving breath, as the wind that guides both people and animals, as maternal comfort, and as a companion through darkness and growth. These mystics demonstrate that the Spirit's communion is not limited by species or circumstance.

Remembering how earlier saints recognized the spiritual bond among God, humans, and the natural world helps explain why I strive to uphold the spiritual tradition of Holy awareness throughout creation. The mystics remind us that every creature, relationship, and moment can become a site of sacred encounter when we stay open to the Spirit's movement. If we seek the pattern of voices across generations, we will begin to discern the larger spiritual truth. By showing that the Spirit is at work within the GHAB, this perspective stands in continuity with that succession of saints who perceived the Spirit's presence in creation and in creaturely relationships; it carries their contemplative insight into our lives.

THE SPIRIT AS BREATH

Augustine of Hippo, one of Christianity's most influential theologians, stands as a witness to the Spirit's work. For Augustine, the Holy Spirit was not just a force, but the very breath of God, making us alive in Christ.[2] His spiritual journey was marked by yearning and restlessness, like a soul searching for its source. In his *Confessions*, Augustine describes the "breath of God" as the animating presence that brings order, comfort, and unity to the wandering heart.[3] He often used the metaphor of wind or breath to describe how the Spirit moves invisibly, giving life to all creatures and drawing them back to their Creator.

THE SPIRIT AS DIVINE WIND

St. Anthony the Great, known as the father of monasticism, serves as another example from the mystical tradition. Retreating into the Egyptian wilderness for prayer and solitude, Anthony often spoke of the Spirit as a wind sensed but not seen. Early accounts describe how Anthony's solitude allowed him to observe animals, wild beasts, and more docile creatures alike, and he saw in their instincts and community the movements of God's Spirit.[4] These animal encounters were more than background characters; they became agents of spiritual lessons in how the Spirit nourishes all living things.

THE SPIRIT AS COMPANION

Consider the writings of St. John of the Cross, a sixteenth-century Spanish mystic who explored the "dark night of the soul." Unlike the common view that equates the dark night only with depression or despair, he described it as a necessary and mysterious journey to union with God; a time when familiar comforts and spiritual assurances are withdrawn. This uncomfortable withdrawal of comforts and assurances awakens the soul to learn to trust and follow God in darkness. It is as if the soul learns to listen, to be patient, and to move with care through the unknown, trusting that the Spirit will ultimately lead to understanding and peace.[5]

The process St. John describes, listening, being patient, and moving carefully through the unknown, mirrors the way healthy bonds are formed and maintained across species. In the GHAB, genuine connection often requires us to let go of our need for control or straightforward answers, and instead to be attentive and open to the Spirit's leading. We may be learning to care for a frightened animal, and the Spirit invites us to be patient and present, believing that understanding and peace will come in time.

THE SPIRIT AS NURTURER

Julian of Norwich's writings give me a sense that she has a deep trust and an open-hearted receptivity to God's love, as I read her testimonies of faith. It seems as though Julian's spiritual posture is marked by patience, calm, and a nurturing presence, as if she's drawing my soul close to her words. Julian's approach to the Spirit doesn't ever seem hurried or forceful. Instead, it is as if she continues to teach her readers that the Spirit's work is gentle and persistent.[6] Indeed, an unhurried, non-forceful presence is a fruit of the Spirit that allows us to be attentive to the needs and rhythms of other creatures. Julian's mystical perspective teaches us that the Spirit's transforming work is rarely rushed; instead, it unfolds gradually, inviting us into deeper relationships of trust and care.

One of the most famous references to the natural world in Julian's writings is her vision of the hazelnut. She writes:

> *And in this God showed me a little thing, the quantity of a hazelnut, lying in the palm of my hand, as it seemed. And it was as round as any ball. I looked upon it with the eye of my understanding, and thought: 'What may this be?' And it was answered generally thus: 'It is all that is made.' I marveled how it might last, for I thought it might suddenly have fallen to nothing for littleness. And I was answered in my understanding: 'It lasts and ever shall, for God loves it. And so have all things their beginning by the love of God.*[7]

According to Julian, the hazelnut she holds is nothing less than *all that is made. This miniature world* could crumble into nothing from sheer vulnerability, yet endures only because it is continually held in being by God's love.

THE SPIRIT AS LIVING BOND

St. Francis of Assisi also serves as a shining example of this shared Spirit at the core of the GHAB. His life of radical simplicity and joy was characterized by an awareness of the Spirit's presence in "brother sun and sister moon,"[8] in birds, wolves, and the poor alike. Francis did not see animals only as symbols but as fellow creatures united under the same Father and animated by the same breath of God. In him, we see how reflective intimacy with Christ naturally fosters attention to animals, land, and the most vulnerable neighbors.

RECOGNITION TO PARTICIPATION TO WITNESS: NOWHERE «SPIRIT» EVERYWHERE

I've found myself returning to this theological symbol I wrote in my journal (see Figure 1 in Appendix B).[9] I realize that placing a mathematical symbol after a discussion on mystery is a deliberate paradox. Like the "coincidence of opposites" described by fifteenth-century mystic Nicholas of Cusa, it points to a grace that no formula can contain.[10] I'm not trying to quantify or limit God's presence; the notation is a theological symbol, not a calculation. It's a pedagogical tool that *invites* contemplation, like a shorthand meant to draw our attention to the vastness of the Spirit's involvement in the world, rather than reduce that mystery to something we can solve.

IMMANENCE AND TRANSCENDENCE: NOWHERE «SPIRIT» EVERYWHERE

Nowhere names all the places that feel empty or forgotten. We might think, "God can't be at work here; this is just a backyard."[11] The Spirit's presence, not our perception, determines a place's significance. The Spirit is both immanent, dwelling within the places and moments we actually experience, and transcendent, surpassing the limits of space and time.

Everywhere represents all of creation. Even if we gathered every place and called that "*everywhere*," the Spirit would still go beyond it. The Spirit isn't just a force within the universe; it also surpasses it. The Spirit is greater than both and is fully present in each ordinary place we inhabit. It is the source and sustainer of all life, and the connecting presence within the GHAB. In that way, the Spirit is like the dashes in the phrase God–human–animal: an invisible "glue" that holds the bond together.

We will never fully explain this mystery with symbols or language. However, naming the Spirit's presence is important because, without it, we can't properly describe the sacred connection that binds God, humans, and animals, a connection often ignored or missing from traditional HAB models.

THE SPIRIT'S FUNCTION UPON OUR PLACES AND EXPERIENCES (P, E)

Building on this kataphatic view, **place** and **experience** (*p*, *e*) are two theological variables that denote the moment when the Spirit is recognized, and all three intersect. Nevertheless, we encounter the Spirit, sometimes without recognizing it as a spiritual event. Every day, we pass through places like homes, grocery stores, clinics, trails, and offices, sharing them and our experiences with others. Yet, we often don't slow down or be mindful of the Spirit's work, so we keep that experience to ourselves.

THE SPIRIT ACTING UPON PLACES AND EXPERIENCES AS THEOLOGICAL VARIABLES

To illustrate how I believe the Spirit works within a single experience, I use a simple theological and relational symbol: $S(p, e)$ means *that a place* (p) and an *experience* (e) are *transformed* or *acted upon* by the Spirit's presence (S). In this model, I *do not* treat S as a number to add or multiply, but rather as a *transformative operator or a function* $f(x, y)$. In simple terms, an operator (or *function*) is not a quantity; it is something (or, in this case, Someone) that *acts on* something else. To clarify, $S(p, e)$ denotes that the Spirit (S) is the active agent who works *upon* and *within* a place (p) and experience (e). The $S(p, e)$ becomes a grace-filled experience.

It is safe to say, the notation does not and cannot "measure" the amount of or absence of spiritual presence; it is a symbolic way of naming the Spirit's relational and transforming action upon and within shared places and experiences.

THE SPIRITUAL EXPERIENCE: S(P, E) = 1

When someone *recognizes* a Spirit-touched experience, we might refer to it as $S(p, e) = 1$: a single "thin place" or spiritual moment, but either way, it is one grace-filled instant in that specific setting (See Figure in Appendix B).

WHEN WE SHARE THE SPIRITUAL EXPERIENCE: S(P, E) = +1

When we choose to share that story with others, it becomes '+1', a *missional* moment. The 'plus one' is not just about telling a story; it is an *intentional* act of bearing witness to the Spirit's presence, which invites others into the narrative.

Viewed this way, the shift from $S(p, e)$ to $S(p, e) = 1$, and then to $S(p, e) = +1$, illustrates a *gradual, mission-focused process* by which we experience and share the already-present Spirit's activity in our lives. In other words, the Spirit is not waiting for our symbols to begin working (See Figure in Appendix B).

THE SPIRIT'S ONGOING WORK

With the Spirit permeating and sustaining all creation, renewal and redemption are not private or individualistic. They have wide-ranging personal, environmental, and cultural implications. The cycles of growth and healing we see in the changing of seasons, the restoration of broken relationships, and the revival of communities all bear witness to the Spirit's ongoing work. The Spirit's activity is not limited to followers of Christ or to moments of prayer. As the very breath of life, the Spirit animates and renews all creatures, human and animal alike. This truth challenges us to seek God's presence and action throughout the whole web of life and to join in the Spirit's work of reconciliation, justice, and renewal wherever we find it. Therefore, let us invite one another to actively participate in the Spirit's mission by engaging in local initiatives that promote environmental sustainability, build community resilience, and foster inclusivity. Humans bear a distinctive calling as image-bearers of God (the *imago Dei*), yet that calling unfolds within a larger community of creatures who, like us, receive their life from God. This uniqueness distinguishes us from other creatures, but it is given not for superiority, but for a deeper responsibility toward them as fellow recipients of God's care.

Sometimes the Spirit offers us a journey that calls for patient endurance and awareness in darkness, and other times it invites a certain level of receptivity and trust. Throughout history, Christian mystics have testified that the Spirit guides, renews, and unites the soul, whether through cautious movement in the shadows or peaceful rest in the light. In either case, the sacred bond we share becomes our means to meaningful companionship.

Just as these mystics experienced the Spirit's presence in their lives and the world around them, I, too, have seen the Spirit at work in deeply personal ways. Their stories, along with my own experiences, remind me that the Spirit's activity is not just in the past but continues today, shaping the GHAB through rhythms and encounters on my journey.

SPIRIT, RELATIONSHIP, AND THE HEART OF THE GHAB

One reason God's Spirit has been given to us is that we need a helper, an advocate, the Paraclete. Jesus promised, "The Advocate, the Holy Spirit, whom the Father will send in my name, will teach you all things and will remind you of everything I have said to you" (Jn. 14:26). We, like the first disciples, are unfinished; we need guidance to walk our paths. That guidance is not only for our own sake. The Spirit's presence is the living heart of the GHAB, drawing us into relationships that cross species boundaries.

In this chapter, I have tried, however imperfectly, to name the Spirit's role in the natural world, giving life to humans, animals, and ecosystems. These are humble attempts to speak of a mystery that will always exceed our language. Yet this mystery is not as abstract as we may think; the reality of the Spirit living in and with us is lived out in particular places, with animals and people. As we move into the next chapter, we will turn more to those lived stories. A *shared* Spirit begets *shared stories.*

QUESTIONS FOR REFLECTION AND PRACTICE

- When you think about the images in this chapter such as the hidden well, Jesus breathing the Spirit on the disciples, the Spirit renewing "the face of the ground," the stories of Winston's visits, the Golden Retriever's hidden pain, and the witness of the mystics, which one most clearly reflects how you have experienced the Spirit in your own life? What does that image invite you to trust or do differently?
- This week, choose *one* ordinary place or relationship where you suspect the Spirit may already be at work. Pause there and pray, "Spirit, guide and help me see who or what needs are here." Afterwards, ask yourself: how did that simple act of recognition change the way I saw the place, the animal, or my own role in the GHAB?

NOTES

1. Sallie McFague, *A New Climate for Theology: God, the World, and Global Warming* (Minneapolis: Fortress Press, 2008), 117.
2. Augustine, *Confessions*, trans. Henry Chadwick (Oxford: Oxford University Press, 1991), 224.
3. Augustine, *Confessions*, 229.
4. Benedicta Ward, *The Sayings of the Desert Fathers: The Alphabetical Collection* (Kalamazoo, MI: Cistercian Publications, 1984), 3–4.
5. St. John of the Cross, *Dark Night of the Soul*, trans. E. Allison Peers (New York: Image Books, 1959), 77–79.
6. Julian of Norwich, *Revelations of Divine Love*, trans. Clifton Wolters (London: Penguin Books, 1998), 138–40.
7. Julian of Norwich, *Revelations of Divine Love*, trans. Clifton Wolters (London: Penguin Books, 1966), 65.

8. Francis of Assisi, "The Canticle of Brother Sun," in *Francis and Clare: The Complete Works*, trans. Regis J. Armstrong and Ignatius C. Brady (Mahwah, NJ: Paulist Press, 1982), 37–38.

9. As shown in Figure 1 of *The Missional Unfolding of the Triune God* (see Appendix B), S(p, e) is already a missional reality, spiritually speaking: a place and an experience quickened by the Spirit. The "+1" does not add anything more spiritual; it simply indicates that the next intentional step of that same grace is symbolically represented as a +1 when we choose to share the story of that Spirit-touched encounter with someone else.

10. Nicholas of Cusa describes the *coincidentia oppositorum* ("coincidence of opposites") as the way in which seemingly contradictory realities, such as maximum and minimum, finite and infinite, are reconciled in God, who transcends the limits of creaturely reason. In Cusa's view, the divine mystery is best approached *not* by resolving all tension, but by recognizing that in God, opposites can coincide without contradiction. See Roman Murawski, "Mathematics and Theology in the Thought of Nicholas of Cusa," *Logica Universalis* 13 (2019): 477–85, accessed January 22, 2026, *https://doi.org/10.1007/s11787-019-00232-2*.

11. Nowhere «Spirit» Everywhere: Scripture affirms that there is "nowhere" outside God's presence; In Acts 17:28, it says, "In him we live and move and have our being." Nowhere «Spirit» Everywhere does not mean the Spirit *is* the world. Instead, it names a God who is truly present to every place and creature, yet still beyond and greater than everything God has made.

7

A SHARED STORY

I'm learning to embrace the art of living imperfectly. Life rarely unfolds in neat black-and-white lines, and most days come in shades of gray. Even so, I continue to lean into God's perfection and steady love. The very life within me, the breath, energy, and imagination that allowed me to write this book, is a gift of God's grace. As I tell the truth about my imperfection, I'm freed from pretending I can hold everything together and can lean more fully into His perfection and steady love. I consider these my "unfinished" places.

That grace is teaching me a different way of seeing myself and the world. I'm also learning to love myself in all my flaws and undesirable places, like my impatience, my fear of not doing enough, and the ways I've overlooked the creatures right beside me. On this path of spiritual growth, animals have not simply stayed in the background of my story; they have become *moving thin places*, companions and teachers through whom, in ways I do not fully understand, God continues to reshape my life. The animals have stood beside me in moments of joy and grief, and in seasons when my own anger, anxiety, or numbness felt louder than God's voice, nudging me toward God when I was lost in my own thoughts. In many ways, they have become friends and guides who help shape my story of faith.

These unfinished places in me are not separate from the rest of this book; they are part of the story I share with the animals and places around me. My imperfect life, like theirs, exists within God's larger story of grace and within the GHAB. It becomes a shared story where grace flows between the Creator and creatures.

This brings us to the heart of this chapter: *We live inside stories, and they live inside us.*

Each of us carries a personal story filled with memories, wounds, hopes, habits, and daily routines. Some stories are familiar, while others are marked by intense moments: the phone call announcing a diagnosis, the night a marriage ended, the miscarriage no one else knew about, the accident that changed a body forever, the job loss that shattered a sense of purpose, the death of a child, a parent sent to prison, or losing a pet who felt like family. These are not just abstract ideas; they are *real* moments we might start to call "chapters" or the "before" and "after," and they often become places where grief, anger, love, and hope live together for a while.

While it can be difficult during tough personal times, our lives also happen within larger stories: generational roles, congregational histories, neighborhood and national political crises, and cultural expectations.

We also share, live, and then narrate our stories that include animals, like the dog who will not leave our side when we are in tears, the horse who learns to trust again after abuse, and the elderly cat whose slow decline forces us to face our limits and choose euthanasia. These are not just emotional side stories; they are GHAB stories.

LOCATING OUR STORIES IN GOD'S STORY

Each of these personal, communal, and animal stories raises another question: *Where do all these stories belong?* Missiologist Michael Goheen says, "To be human is to be a part of a story, and to understand its beginning and its ending."[1] He argues that we truly understand who we are only when we place our lives within God's larger story: creation, fall, redemption, and new creation. In another context, he emphasizes that the journey of knowing Christ runs through our ordinary human experience, inviting us to take the depth and complexity of our own lives seriously.[2] In other words, we come to know Christ not by stepping outside our ordinary lives, but by paying close attention to them.

An animal's presence, as part of our own, adds depth to how we interpret and share our story. As we focus on the resilience, loyalty, and companionship of animals, the Spirit uses their lives to remind us of the biblical story of the God who cares for sparrows and lilies, donkeys and ravens, and who calls us to share in that care. This is the GHAB in action.

My goal here is not just to argue that animals can help our spirituality; that belief runs throughout this entire book. Instead, this chapter highlights how the stories we create and live, as humans and animals, can become sacred stories that testify to God's grace. Think of these stories as thin places that offer glimpses of God's grace and reveal the creative flow of the GHAB. We celebrate God's presence in creation while honoring the distinction between the Creator and the created; we worship the Giver, not just the gifts.

KATAPHATIC AND APOPHATIC SPIRITUALITY

Christian spirituality has long recognized that we come to know God in two complementary ways. One way, called *kataphatic*, is through what we can see and speak about: stories, images, creation, relationships, and everyday details of our lives. In this way, we focus on how God is *revealed* in the world and in Scripture, through concrete signs, words, and experiences that help us identify God's presence. The other method, called *apophatic*, involves knowing God by revering what *we cannot fully explain*: not a complete absence, but God's sacred mystery—a presence too deep and vast for our language—his hidden work beneath the surface of our lives. The stories in this chapter embrace *both approaches*: they present real moments with animals and creation that we can point to and say, "God was here," while also leaving room for the parts we do not know or cannot answer.

The GHAB itself becomes a kind of kataphatic anchor and apophatic mystery. On one hand, an animal's touch, gaze, or steady presence is a visible sign of God's closeness in a relationship we can see and describe. On the other hand, we can never fully understand an animal's inner life or all that God is doing through that bond; there is always more than we can explain.

By paying attention to these stories, we begin to see that the GHAB is not just an extra detail at the edge of our faith, but a part of how God is writing redemption into the world. For example, when a dog curls up beside us as we pray after a hard day, the *kataphatic* way sees this as a visible sign of God's nearness in an ordinary moment we can describe and remember. At the same time, there's a depth to this comfort that we cannot fully explain. It offers us peace and a sense of being held, in more than just fur and warmth. That is the *apophatic* dimension: the hidden work of God's Spirit beneath the surface. Together, these ways of knowing teach us to see the GHAB as one of the places where God's redeeming love is both visible and working in mysterious ways.

THE SPIRIT'S TIMELESS GIFTS: HINDSIGHT, MINDFULNESS, AND DISCERNMENT IN OUR SACRED STORIES

Storytelling isn't limited to ancient history; it influences our lives today. We scroll through social media stories, retell headlines, exchange family memories, and share testimonies at church. Whether we realize it or not, most of our conversations involve stories, and God often meets us there.

I frequently notice this when someone drops a dog off for boarding. Initially, it seems like small talk: "She's getting older," "He hates thunderstorms," "Please make sure he has his blanket; it helps him settle." But as the owner stays longer, their story deepens. They remember the dog who stayed by their side during a divorce. What begins as care instructions turns into a story about loyalty, fear, comfort, and how God has met them through their dog's steady presence. In hindsight, what first seemed like logistics often reveals itself as a living record of the GHAB.

As people of faith, the question is not *whether* we tell stories, but *how* we share them. When we prayerfully reflect on past seasons, observe what God is doing now, and trust more fully, our stories become places where the Spirit actively works. In all of this, we do not rely solely on our own insight; we respond to gifts the Spirit has already given us.

Hindsight, mindfulness, and discernment are gifts from God. They are not signs of our cleverness or control, but expressions of God's generosity. As James reminds us, "Every good and perfect gift is from above, coming down from the Father of the heavenly lights, who does not change like shifting shadows" (Jas. 1:17). Recognizing these gifts as coming from God and not from our own achievement allows us to accept them with humility and gratitude.

In the following sections, we explore how the Spirit uses hindsight, mindfulness, and discernment not only to shape our faith but also to help us see the GHAB more clearly in our own stories.

THE GIFT OF HINDSIGHT

Hindsight is the Spirit-enabled practice of looking back to see God's movements in our lives. It helps us step outside the swirl of our emotions and view our story within a larger story. Without it, we can easily become stuck in regret, confusion, or self-reproach. Scripture often calls God's people to remember. In Deuteronomy 8:2, God encourages Israel to "remember how the Lord your God led you all the way in the wilderness." They are encouraged to recall the twists and turns of their journey, how God humbled and tested them, and how trust was built along the way. We understand these insights because their story has been retold and valued over generations.

The same is true in our own lives. When we practice hindsight, whether through journaling, praying over old seasons with a trusted friend, or recalling the animals who have walked with us, we begin to notice patterns of God's faithfulness. We might remember a scared dog that helped us face our fears, or a dying horse whose story revealed God's compassion through a community's care. Hindsight doesn't erase the pain, but it shows us where God's presence was at work, even when we couldn't see it at the time. It also helps us trace the GHAB through our past, recognizing how God used animals to sustain us when human words have fallen short.

An example of this is Joseph, who, reflecting on his brothers' betrayal, said, "You intended to harm me, but God intended it for good to accomplish what is now being done, the saving of many lives" (Gen. 50:20). In hindsight,

Joseph understood that God's greater purposes were at work in his suffering. The same applies to us. By examining our past with God, including our stories with animals, we can find healing, courage, and a clearer understanding of how our lives fit into God's larger story.

Hindsight, then, is not nostalgia. It is purposeful remembrance that reveals God's faithfulness and shapes our spiritual growth. When we do this prayerfully, especially in community, we discover that the God who was faithful then remains steadfast today. Our past can become more than just memory; it is transformed into a foundation of hope as we begin to see each person's, each community's, and even each ecosystem's story, including our own and the stories of the animals we love, as part of God's greater narrative.

If hindsight helps us learn from the past, mindfulness helps us *receive* the present.

THE GIFT OF MINDFULNESS

Mindfulness keeps us grounded in the present moment. It involves fully experiencing everyday activities: washing dishes, walking the dog, driving to work, or sitting in a waiting room. When we are truly present, we are less controlled by past regrets or future worries. In this grounded state, we can begin to notice how the Spirit unexpectedly transforms ordinary moments into holy ones.

Consider Paul's prayer in Ephesians 3:19: "and to know this love that surpasses knowledge—that you may be filled to the measure of all the fullness of God." Paul isn't just asking us to be filled in a vague way; he's urging us to understand Christ's love so deeply that, as that love takes root in us, we are filled to overflowing with the very fullness of God, like baskets filled with bread after the feeding of the five thousand (Matt. 14:13–21; cf. Mk.

6:30–44; Lk. 9:10–17; Jn. 6:1–14). In those moments, the Spirit affirms our identity as beloved children (Rom. 8:16) and nurtures in us the fruits of love, joy, peace, patience, kindness, goodness, faithfulness, gentleness, and self-control (Gal. 5:22–23). These aren't just *private* virtues; they influence how we treat the people and animals around us, how we listen, and how we forgive.

Pentecost in Acts 2 serves as another clear example. The disciples were simply gathered when the Spirit stepped in. Their ordinary meeting turned into an extraordinary encounter: "tongues of fire" appeared (Acts 2:3), and "all of them were filled with the Holy Spirit" (Acts 2:4). In that upper room, an everyday gathering became a sacred moment. Their simple act of coming together before God opened them to receive what the Spirit was eager to give.

But what if they had been too distracted or too busy to gather at all, such as mending nets by the lake, rushing to the market, or staying home to handle family worries instead of waiting and praying together? Yet in our lives, *mindlessness* often seems unimportant, yet it can be just as spiritually dangerous. On an average day, it shows up as rushing, scrolling, and multitasking, and can become numbing. We feed the dog on autopilot, ignore the bird singing outside our window, and move from one emotionally draining task to another without prayer or gratitude. Over time, this daily mindlessness dulls our awareness of God and the creatures around us, making it harder to notice the GHAB that is already present.

Left unchecked on a larger scale, habitual mindlessness can harm the community. When entire communities stop paying attention, we tend to drift toward practices like factory farming, habitat destruction, and careless consumption, not always out of deliberate cruelty but often out of neglect.

In a rural community, a private land development slowly began to change the landscape. What seemed on paper like a simple excavation project grew larger over time, transforming the terrain and affecting both people and wildlife. Neighbors worried about cracks in buildings, increased heavy-truck traffic on narrow roads, and potential effects on their wells and local waterways. What appears, on the surface, to be an individual decision about how to use one parcel of land actually becomes, in practice, a shared story for people, animals, and the land itself. How we tell the story of that place will either mask or reveal what's really happening.

Cultivating mindfulness begins to reverse that drift into distraction and numbness. As a spiritual practice, mindfulness invites us to slow down, notice God's presence, and respond with reverence. When we intentionally invite the Spirit into our routines, pausing before we eat, genuinely greeting a dog or cat, noticing an insect on the windowsill, we become more present to God and more compassionate toward all creation. Everyday moments become opportunities for spiritual encounter and for honoring the GHAB.

THE GIFT OF DISCERNMENT

As we turn our gaze toward what lies ahead, the Spirit offers the gift of discernment, a forward-leaning peace that helps us face the unknown with confidence. Discernment is more than making good decisions; it is learning to recognize God's leading amid many competing voices, including our own fears and desires.

A modern example of this kind of discernment comes from the life of Dallas Willard. After completing college and being ordained as a Baptist minister, Willard realized that his learning journey was far from over. He felt profoundly unprepared in his understanding of God and the human soul, to the point that he worried about unintentionally misleading those he served. Rather than pretending to *know enough*, he followed a deep, uneasy conviction that God was inviting him to keep learning. That inner nudge led him into graduate studies in philosophy.

Through this season of study, Willard began to sense a specific call emerging: his place of service would be both the university and the church. He later described a clear, guiding word from God: "If you stay in the churches, the university will be closed to you; but if you stay in the university, the churches will be open to you."[3] On the surface, this seemed backwards. Shouldn't the ministry stay inside the church walls? And yet, like God's words in Isaiah 55:8–9, "My thoughts are not your thoughts, neither are your ways my ways...," this call invited him to trust beyond what he could immediately understand. Stepping out in faith, he accepted a position at the University of Southern California and spent decades serving both students and churches.

Discernment in our lives may not come through such a dramatic sentence, but it is often seen as the same deep, settling peace. It grows as we:

1. **Remember** how God has been faithful in the past (hindsight),
2. **Notice** what the Spirit is doing in the present (mindfulness), and
3. **Listen** for how God may be inviting us to step forward (discernment).

These are not techniques we master; we practice them. Discernment develops as we stay rooted in prayer, saturated in Scripture, and realistically mindful of our circumstances. Willard sometimes spoke of "intelligent alertness,"[4] paying careful attention to our lives with God, rather than drifting through them on autopilot. As we do this, the Spirit often provides an assurance, a sense of "this is the way," that does not remove all risk but gives courage to walk in it.

We see a picture of hindsight, mindfulness, and discernment linked to the story of the two disciples on the road to Emmaus (Lk. 24:13–35). Confused and heartbroken, they walked away from Jerusalem, talking about all that had happened to Jesus. They remembered his ministry and the hope they had placed in him as Redeemer. They also recounted the strange reports of an empty tomb and angels' messages (Lk. 24:19–24). Their disappointment and confusion are palpable: they are "slow of heart to believe all that the prophets have declared" (Lk. 24:25).

A stranger joins them on the road. They do not recognize him, but he patiently walks with them and reminds them: "Beginning with Moses and all the Prophets, he explained to them what was said in all the Scriptures concerning himself" (Lk. 24:27). It will not be long before their story begins to take on a new shape.

As evening comes, the disciples move from hindsight to mindfulness. They pay attention to the present moment and invite the stranger to stay with them (Lk. 24:28–29). Around the table, in the simple act of breaking bread, everything shifts: "He took bread, gave thanks, broke it and began to give it to them. Then their eyes were opened, and they recognized him" (Lk. 24:30–31). Their hearts had already been "burning within us while he talked with us on the road and opened the Scriptures to us" (Lk. 24:32), but it is in this concrete, sensory moment that discernment finally flowers. They know who he is and what they must do.

If the story had unfolded differently, like if they had refused to remember, to listen, or to invite him in, their confusion might have hardened into despair. Instead, hindsight, mindfulness, and discernment work together. The past is reframed, the present becomes a place of encounter, and the future opens into mission as they hurry back to share the news.

To recap: **hindsight** reframes the past, **mindfulness** reveals the present, and **discernment** helps us take our next faithful step. These three spiritual practices allow the Spirit to reshape our stories into testimonies rather than into avoidance or regret, and they also train us to notice and respond to the GHAB in ways more aligned with God's reconciling work.

As the Spirit transforms our personal stories, our perceptions and responses to the world around us also expand. This includes our relationships with humans and with the rest of creation. When we are mindful enough to see God's generosity and creativity reflected in animals, we gain a vital relationship for our spiritual formation. Their presence becomes part of how we learn Christlike love and how we tell God's story. And the way we tell God's story is not something we hold tightly to ourselves; it is like opening our arms wide for an embrace, so that others can step into the circle of God's grace with us.

ANIMALS AS INSTRUMENTS OF SPIRITUAL FORMATION

When we think about spiritual formation, we often envision church services, Bible studies, or disciplines such as prayer and fasting. We may not immediately think of dogs, horses, or rabbits. Yet animals often become part of the path God chooses to shape our hearts and habits.

Spiritual formation, in Paul's language, is about being re-oriented and re-habituated, learning to live a new kind of life in Christ. He writes, "Since, then, you have been raised with Christ, set your hearts on things above, where Christ is, seated at the right hand of God. Set your minds on things above, not on earthly things" (Col. 3:1–2).

Paul then describes what this re-orientation looks like in practice, calling believers to put off old patterns and put on new ones (Col. 3:7–8, 12–14). This is not merely an inner change in belief; it is a transformation of what drives our emotions, shapes our evaluations, and guides our daily habits; for example, how quickly we grow angry or forgive, what we count as necessary, how we use our time and money, and how we treat those who depend on us, including animals.

Animals can be included in this process. They serve as *living reminders* of the person we are becoming in Christ. You might be wondering, "What does this even mean?" I'm glad you asked.

ANIMALS NATURALLY CREATE SITUATIONS FOR US TO RESPOND

In everyday encounters, animals draw out habits already within us and give the Spirit concrete contexts in which to work. A fearful stray dog that repeatedly pulls away or hides invites us to practice patience rather than irritation. A stubborn donkey that resists being led exposes our impulse to control and offers us the chance to learn a calmer, humbler way of guiding. A dying horse that gathers an entire community into compassion, courage, and shared grief draws us out of isolation and into a circle of care. In these moments, animals function like mirrors, reflecting who we are in practice more than in theory: when a dog cowers at our raised voice or relaxes under our calm touch, or when a horse tenses at our impatience but softens as we slow our breathing, we can see the gap between what we confess and how we actually move through the world. Each interaction becomes a new chance to choose differently and respond with faithfulness rather than withdrawal, gentleness rather than harshness, and self-control rather than impulsive reactions. None of this replaces the central role of Scripture, prayer, and the church as the primary, God-ordained means of grace. Scripture, prayer, and the church remain the primary, God-ordained means of grace. For example, animals do not teach doctrine; rather, the Spirit uses our encounters with them to *catalyze* the practice of Christlike patience, gentleness, and care. Seeing it this way, animals become part of the network of relationships through which the Spirit re-orients our hearts and re-habituates our daily lives.

When we invite animals into our homes or onto our land, they rarely remain *just* pets. They become part of the interconnected relationships that God uses to shape us.

This is especially true at home, a shared space where stories unfold. It's often where our most genuine selves emerge and where our habits, both good and bad, are most visible. When we bring dogs, cats, and other animals into that intimate setting, it opens a new level of spiritual growth with God, ourselves, others, and the animals. God's Spirit, which gives life to animals, reveals glimpses of the Creator through them: peace, love, faithfulness, and companionship (Gen. 1:30; 2:7). In many ways, God's Spirit uses home life, involving both humans and animals, to show how He provides for and cares for us.

Even Jesus pointed us to animals and the natural world as signs of God's care. He spoke of sparrows, lilies, ravens, donkeys, and the grasses of the field (Matt. 10:29; Lk. 12:28), not as scenery, but as witnesses to the Father's provision. Remembering Jesus' generosity toward these creatures can strengthen our confidence. Trust grows as we pray, ask for what we need, and then notice how God meets us; sometimes, through human hands and other times, through the presence of an animal.

MORNINGS WITH TWIG

Some mornings, before the sun rises, Twig decides to join me as I stumble around looking for a coffee cup. He doesn't always want to leave his big, brown, fluffy bed, but on those days when he does, he enters the living room and waits while I make coffee. As soon as I settle into the recliner and lean back, he knows the routine. He jumps onto the footrest, curls against my legs, and forms a ball. Then I feel ready to relax: I have my dog, my Bible, and my coffee, and together we watch the first light break through the living room window. In that simple moment when we share warmth, stillness, and a view of the coming day, I can almost feel God's presence. Twig isn't *just* in the room; he *is part* of how God teaches me to be present, to listen, and to accept the gift of a new morning. It's in this morning ritual where the GHAB seems to take on a very ordinary, yet holy shape in my home.

DONA BERTARELLI'S STORY: FROM SAILING TO ADVOCACY

Dona Bertarelli has spent much of her life on the water. On one 30-day voyage around Cape Horn aboard her maxi-trimaran (very large) sailboat, she woke each day to a world that felt both fragile and immense. She remembers "pastel skies, snow-capped mountains and glaciers tumbling to the sea, illuminated with pink hues, while thousands of birds danced overhead."[5] The scene was breathtaking, as it unfolded over heavy seas, punishing waves, and relentless headwinds. Out there, the ocean was not scenery; it was a force that could cradle or crush.

Those weeks at sea changed the way she saw the world. Sailing demanded constant attention: reading the sky, feeling the wind shift, listening to the hull and rigging for signs of strain. "There's no forcing your way through the ocean," she has said. "You need to read the elements, respond to subtle changes, and think several steps ahead." That posture, one that is attentive, responsive, and humble, began to shape how she thought about the planet itself.

As she learned more about the health of the ocean, the beauty she had experienced at Cape Horn became harder to separate from the brokenness she saw elsewhere. She learned that high seas beyond national borders cover nearly half the planet, yet remain largely unprotected. She read research showing steep declines in marine life, more frequent coral reef bleaching, and fish stocks pushed beyond their limits. The same waters that had carried her boat and held those "pastel skies" were under intense pressure from overfishing, warming, acidification, and pollution.

For Dona, information alone was not enough. She believed that people protect what they understand and fight for what they feel connected to. She began telling ocean stories through interviews, speaking engagements, and visual projects that used photography and film to stimulate imagination and empathy. She became a leading voice in the global effort to protect "30x30": the goal of safeguarding at least 30 percent of the ocean by 2030. Her advocacy is not simply about policy; it arises from that sense of vulnerability at sea and the conviction that the ocean is a vital life-support system for all life on earth.

When Dona describes the sea as "a space for reflection, for clarity, an almost spiritual connection that grounds me," she echoes a truth at the heart of this book: creation is not just a backdrop. It is a place of encounter, responsibility, and call. Offshore sailing taught her to use resources carefully, like food, fuel, and energy, and also to notice what was used, wasted, or truly necessary. That same attentiveness followed her back to land, where she began to ask what kind of future the oceans, and the people and creatures who depend on them, will have.

Her story offers a living picture of the *missio Dei*. God's mission is not only to reconcile individual souls, but to restore and sustain the whole creation. When Dona speaks up for the ocean, she is, often without using this language, joining that mission to resist exploitation, seek justice, and tend to a part of the world God loves. Her sailing, advocacy, and storytelling become acts of stewardship, practical ways of participating in God's work to heal what has been damaged.

In Dona's story, we glimpse a shared story: the ocean's vulnerability, our dependence on it, and God's call to care. It reminds us that loving God and loving neighbor now includes loving the seas that connect every coastline on earth. As stewards, we are invited to respond with humility, love, and action, recognizing that the health of the oceans reflects the health of all creation and that our participation matters in God's ongoing work. In this way, even the vast relationship between humans and the sea is drawn into the GHAB. It shows God's care, human responsibility, and the lives of countless creatures intersecting.

PEARL'S STORY: SUGAR, BLOOD, AND THE BREATH OF GOD

A tragedy struck when Pearl, our fifteen-year-old white Tennessee Walking Horse, gave birth to her foal around 9 p.m. The placenta did not separate from the uterus. When the foal was born, it tore the placenta loose and brought Pearl's uterus with it. She began to hemorrhage. Our regular equine veterinarian was too busy to come, so I called another. By the time a vet from Tennessee Equine Hospital arrived, Pearl was cold and clammy, her uterus lying in the mud and manure, her tiny, long-legged foal standing beside her near-lifeless body.

As we waited, six neighbors had gathered behind our barn, helping in any way they could. They saw me cry and lay bloody, prayerful hands on Pearl's neck. They tried to coax the foal to nurse, but he seemed too stunned to respond. Wide-eyed and shaky, he moved as if the ground were waves beneath him. One neighbor suggested applying creamy peanut butter to Pearl's nipples to attract him. We rubbed it on, and slowly he began to sniff, then hunt with his nose. His lips finally latched on, and an audible sigh of relief was heard, yet mixed with the fear that Pearl might not live long enough to keep feeding him.

The vet placed a halter and lead rope on Pearl and told us she had to stand. All of us pushed and pulled the dying mare until she somehow made it to her feet. He then asked for ten pounds of sugar to shrink the swollen uterus. Another neighbor ran home and returned with her last bag. The vet poured sugar over the exposed tissue, waited as it shrank, then rinsed it with bags of saline before forcing the uterus back inside. He held the opening closed with his hand, hoping Pearl's body wouldn't push it out again.

While he worked, one neighbor held "the twitch" on Pearl's nose so she wouldn't move. Another gripped the halter; another had the lead rope. Others stroked Pearl's neck, kept the foal from wandering, or simply stood there, praying. Our group of friends became a second and third set of hands for the doctor.

"She probably won't make it to see morning," the veterinarian finally said. "Nine times out of ten, she doesn't." It was 2:30 a.m., nearly six hours since the foal had been born. My filthy, exhausted, beautiful neighbors and the weary vet went home, all of them smelling of blood.

The gates behind the barn were streaked with it, the same blood that had covered our hands as we tried to help. Pieces of placenta we had torn away lay scattered in the dirt. There was nothing more we could do. We left

Pearl and her foal standing together in the stall and went to bed, expecting to lose her by morning.

When I woke a few hours later, I didn't want to look in the stall. I pictured Pearl's body on the ground and forced myself to check on what I assumed would now be an orphaned foal.

But there she was, still standing beside her foal, life back in her eyes.

I called the vet, and he was stunned. Pearl and her foal spent a week in the hospital, where Betadine flushes rinsed away the undissolved sugar, mud, and manure. The foal was treated for infection and given a good prognosis. Pearl had beaten the odds.

Our neighbors still remember the helplessness, panic, and grief of that night. They also remember the veterinarian's care and skill, and how neighbors gave whatever they had, like sugar, strength, time, and presence, in order to help a suffering horse and her colt. Ultimately, they recall that there was no human reason for Pearl's survival. Whenever we see one another, they still ask after "the miracle horse."

Though none of us could do much on our own for a mare who was bleeding out, together we offered what we had, and God did what we could not. We all knew who the true Hero was: the One who gives all creation the breath of life.

Over time, Pearl's story has become a cherished testament to the enduring power of community and faith—a living witness to how divine grace, human compassion, and the love of an animal can be woven into one shared story.

These stories, Twig's companionship, Dona's love for the sea, Pearl's near-death experience and healing, trace a shared story of trust, gratitude, humility, and calling. They show that spiritual formation occurs not only in church pews or private devotions but also in a recliner, in a stall, and in open water. In each, the GHAB takes on a particular shape: a dog on a footrest, a sailor on the sea with creatures beneath the surface, a horse and foal surrounded by praying neighbors.

Ultimately, a shared story is never neat or simple. It's as if it rejects the illusion that any of us can live a clean, self-contained narrative in which everything makes sense, and nothing spills over onto others. Instead, by God's grace, our stories hold beauty and brokenness together like answered prayers and aching questions, or faith and confusion. Some moments are clear enough to be seen as gifts from God; others stay wrapped in mystery. *Both* belong in our life with God.

Twig's companionship, Dona's love for the sea, and Pearl's near-death and healing each show a different face of the GHAB. Twig draws the bond into the silence of an ordinary morning, where a dog's warm body and shared stillness become a way for God to teach me grounded presence. Dona widens the bond to a global horizon, where a sailor's attentiveness to wind, water, and birds grows into advocacy for oceans and the countless creatures who depend on them. Pearl's story gathers the bond into a bloody stall at midnight, where her foal, a veterinarian, and a circle of neighbors stand together between life and death, offering what they can while God does what they cannot. In each of these, God, humans, and animals are not separate stories but one of vulnerability and grace.

Yet shared stories serve more than comfort; they also reveal hard truths. As our lives become intertwined with animals and places, we begin to see our limits, our wounds, and the harm we have caused to one another and to creation. To tell the whole story, we must face both the beauty of the bond *and* its fractures. That's where we turn next: to *A Shared Wound.*

QUESTIONS FOR REFLECTION AND PRACTICE

- Which story or scene in this chapter most closely mirrors a chapter in your life? Twig's morning companionship, Dona's time at sea, Pearl's near-death and healing, or one of your own memories with an animal? How might you retell that story now as part of God's larger story of grace, holding together both its beauty and its brokenness, and recognizing it as part of the GHAB?
- This week, set aside a few minutes to practice *hindsight, mindfulness, and discernment,* and sit with *one* human–animal story from your life. *Look back* and *ask,* "Where might God have been at work *in me, in this animal, and between us?*" Notice what the Spirit might have been doing in that relationship. Ask yourself how God might be inviting you *now* to take a faithful step forward because of what you've seen.

NOTES

1. Michael W. Goheen, The Church and Its Vocation, Kindle ed. (Grand Rapids, MI: Eerdmans, 2014), preface, XIV.
2. Goheen, The Church and Its Vocation, 45.
3. "About Dallas," Dallas Willard Center, accessed June 1, 2025, *https://dwillard.org/about-dallas.*
4. Dallas Willard Center, "About Dallas."
5. John Steele, "Hope Catches a Tailwind," Nautilus, June 6, 2025, *https://nautil.us/hope-catches-a-tailwind-1215966/.*

8

A SHARED WOUND

This section includes a practical-theological interpretation of Genesis 3. For many of us, Genesis 3 has been understood mainly as a story of blame and separation: a serpent deceives, humans make a disastrous choice, and everything falls apart. In that interpretation, the human–animal encounter is seen primarily as the moment when sin "entered the world" (see Gen. 3; Rom. 5:12), and that moment shapes how we perceive everything else, ourselves, animals, and the land, as primarily broken. However, this is just one way to tell the story. What follows offers a practical-theological perspective on Genesis 3, focusing on the relationships woven throughout the text rather than on blame alone. If we listen more closely, Genesis 3 reveals a deep wound that runs through the GHAB, a fracture in the way God, humans, and other creatures are meant to belong together.

Even within Genesis 3, the God who pronounces judgment does not withdraw from His creatures. The same chapter that speaks of thorns, thistles, and painful toil (Gen. 3:17–18) also shows God clothing the humans in their shame (Gen. 3:21). His love continues even in a fractured world, and even as the God–human–animal bond bears the marks of that fracture.

This shared brokenness also hints at a common hope. The same God who clothes humans in their shame (Gen. 3:21) and continues to speak to them is the God who later feeds Elijah through ravens, preserves Jonah's life in a great fish, and enters Jerusalem not on a warhorse but on a humble donkey. Throughout Scripture, animals don't leave God's story after Eden; they remain present alongside His people. When a raven brings bread (1 Kgs. 17:4-6), a fish saves a prophet from drowning (Jn. 1:17; 2:1, 10), or a donkey carries Jesus on the way to the Cross (Matt. 21:1-9), we are reminded that God's care for humanity is expressed within, not separate from, the wider creation. These scenes are not evidence that animals share the same covenant status or salvific role as humans; rather, they show God's *providential use of and care for his creatures as he works out his purposes in the world.* Even after the fall, these stories remind us that God has not abandoned his creatures or his world; his care continues to move through more-than-human neighbors.

A DOG, A PAIR OF SHOES, AND A DIFFERENT ENDING

When I was sixteen, working at Pet Health Center, a man brought in his dog, not for treatment, but to have him euthanized. The dog had chewed up his favorite pair of shoes. That was the offense. As he handed over the leash and walked out, I remember thinking, "This can't be happening." A living creature was about to die over leather and laces.

Thankfully, that story did not end the way the man intended. The veterinarian refused to euthanize the dog. Instead, a staff member found him a new home, sending him off with a half-joking warning: "Now, don't chew up any more shoes." What could have been a thoughtless act of cruelty became an unexpected act of mercy.

In that exam room, I saw two stories at once: one in which an animal's life is disposable when it inconveniences us and another in which someone chooses to protect that life instead. *Both* stories are possible within our vulnerabilities, but only one begins to move us toward healing. In the first, the GHAB collapses into power and use; in the second, it becomes a small site of repair, where an animal's future and a human conscience are *both* redirected.

GUARDIANS OF THE NIGHT: PSI AND PARIS

Years later, I met that wound differently, this time in my own home. Our Miniature Schnauzers, Psi and Paris, were so vocal that they were often louder than I preferred. I used to cradle Psi's muzzle in my hand when she launched into a barking fit and whisper, "You know Miniature Schnauzers don't bark," as if saying it softly could make it accurate.

One night, deep in sleep, I was jolted awake by Psi's low growl and an urgent bark. It wasn't her usual tantrum; it was focused. I stumbled out of bed and opened the bedroom door. Psi and Paris shot past me, racing down the hallway toward the study at the far side of the house.

Then their barking exploded.

Peeking through the curtain, I saw three men dismantling the window pane that led into the study. My heart pounded as I called 9-1-1. Before the police arrived, Psi and Paris, two dogs barely ankle-high, had already done their work. Their relentless barking sent the intruders fleeing through the backyard. In their rush to escape, the men kicked through our six-foot privacy fence as if it were made of cardboard.

The same noise I had spent years trying to hush had become an alarm system I thanked God for. In that chaos, our little dogs became guardians of the night. They turned a shared human–animal vulnerability into a moment of protection and grace. In their own way, they stood in the breach of the GHAB, as if they were using their species-specific gifts to shield the humans they loved.

HARRY'S STORY AND FRIENDSHIP WITH AN UNEXPECTED CREATURE

Not all wounds are loud or evident at first glance; some are unseen and stretched over long periods. I learned this in an eight-by-eight-foot room in Kuwait.

My first deployment as a young, enlisted Security Forces member was at Al Jaber in 2002. Some days, I was posted in a tower; other days, I was assigned to a small underground room with a low dirt ceiling. During twelve-hour shifts, I sat alone, alert, and was not allowed to leave my post. Food was brought to me by another guard. The only way to see outside was through the barrel of my rifle, resting just above the ground.

After weeks of this, the isolation and monotony began to wear me down. I finished the word-find book I brought, and my thoughts started circling in anxious loops. I felt myself slipping into a kind of despair.

Then, one night, I noticed a gray mouse in the corner, looking at me. He sat there for a long time, watching, and I watched him. He would scurry away and then return, night after night, as if checking on me. I decided to call him Harry.

Being from the South, feeding others, whether human or animal, comes naturally. So I asked the guard who brought my meals to include a plastic cup of peanut butter. I didn't tell him it was for a mouse. I placed the cup in the corner and waited. Slowly, Harry crept out, sniffed, and began to eat with his tiny front teeth. He loved it. Watching him, something in me softened.

Harry became a tiny light in that dark, dusty cell. I don't usually like mice, but I loved Harry. Knowing he would appear each night gave me something to look forward to; his presence made me feel less alone. I'm not sure what happened to him after I redeployed, but I still hope that, in his own mouse-sized way, his needs were met as he helped meet mine. I see Harry as another unexpected way God met me in a place of fatigue and fear; he was a creature most people would ignore or try to kill, but the Lord offered me companionship and comfort. I learned that there is no place that is too distant, hidden, or lonely for his love to reach. In that underground bunker, the GHAB did not look grand or heroic; it looked like shared survival between a tired Airman and a hungry mouse. In a different key, Harry's presence echoed the God who clothed the first humans in their shame (Gen. 3:21): a quiet provision in a desolate place, reminding me that divine care can arrive through the smallest of creatures.

LISTENING TO ANIMALS ON THEIR OWN TERMS

The shared wound I have been describing isn't limited to crises; it also shows up in the simple ways we speak about animals. Our everyday language can either deepen the divide between us or help start to bridge it. Even brief spoken-word choices influence us, encouraging greater mindfulness. Words shape our stories, and over time, those stories affect how we see God, ourselves, and animals. One way this happens is through anthropomorphism, the giving of human traits to animals. Anthropomorphism can soften our hearts, but it can also tempt us to project our longings onto animals and overlook their *actual* needs and limits.

I've noticed this tension with Winston. During one visit, a staff member at a facility rubbed his neck and said, "He just loves all this attention. He'd be happy being hugged all day." From the outside, it seemed that way. Winston stood still, ears relaxed, head slightly lowered as people gathered around him. In that moment, the story in the room—"He loves all this attention" was a classic example of *naive projection*: a human desire laid over his body without listening to what he was *actually* saying.

But as I watched more closely, I began to notice other signals. His breathing grew shallow, his eyes kept flicking toward the door, and his tail, usually loose and swinging, began to twitch rapidly. This is often how he tells me it is time for a bathroom break, but that day those same signals also told me he was ready to leave, whether for the restroom or simply because he was done visiting. The more people leaned in, the more he shifted his weight away from the center of the circle, pressing against my side. To most people in the room, his stillness read as contentment, but for Winston, it was his way of saying, "I'm done visiting."

In that moment, I had a choice. I could agree with the comforting narrative, "He loves all this attention," or I could honor what his body was actually telling me. I stepped in, thanked the group, and said, "We're going to give Winston a little break," then walked him outside. Once we were away from the crowd, he sighed and looked around, as if to say, "I'm done for today." I thanked the staff for the visit, and we headed home so he could do what he loves most after a long day, roll in his favorite dusty circle on the ground.

Looking back, that visit with Winston helped me move from naive projection to informed empathy: instead of repeating, "He loves this," I let his species-specific signals guide my response, and in doing so, I could actually care for him rather than for my own comforting story.

I saw how easy it was to use a human-centered story to ignore his limits, to keep telling myself, "He loves being the center of attention," rather than admit that his body was signaling, "I need a break." The staff's affection for Winston was sincere, and their words came from love, but without paying attention to his cues, that love could quickly turn into pressure. Their words would have hidden his stress rather than help ease it.

Stories like this keep me honest. They remind me that while it is good to speak tenderly to and about our animals, those words must be checked against what their bodies and behavior truly communicate. When our metaphors align with an animal's real needs, they deepen compassion. When they only reflect our own desires, they risk wounding the very creatures we say we love. The GHAB is not only written on our hearts and minds in our grand gestures, but also in the discipline of listening to an animal *on its own terms.*

EMPATHY AND CREATURELY DIFFERENCE

Sometimes, I describe animals in human terms, saying, for example, that a dog is "jealous," a cat is "offended," or a horse is "patient." I find this practice helpful because it can spark our imaginations and soften our hearts. When we recognize parts of ourselves in an animal, our empathy often deepens, and we become more attentive to *the animal itself*—its posture, mood, and way of being with us.

At the same time, it's important to remember that animals are not simply reflections of us. They are their own kind of creatures, with species-specific ways of perceiving, relating, and communicating. When I anthropomorphize, I do so as a spiritual and imaginative practice, sometimes playfully, not as a scientific claim that animals are just little humans. I agree that anthropomorphizing can be meaningful, but it needs to be done mindfully and with respect for each species' own qualities.

I hope this language helps us view animals as companions and, in a limited, creaturely sense, as our friends in God's creation, deserving of attention and care, without losing sight of the difference between their unique, God-given nature and our own. Through this lens, anthropomorphism becomes *less* about remaking animals in *our* image and *more* about accepting God's invitation to notice his love reflected in all creatures. All in all, it's important to avoid careless language that pushes us farther from them and the rest of creation.

ANTHROPOMORPHISM, PRACTICED WITH DISCERNMENT

Rather than treating anthropomorphism as simply good or bad, it may help to see it as a progression. At one end is *naive projection*, where we read our own desires onto an animal and ignore its real limits. In the middle is *careful observation*, where we learn what a species actually needs and how it communicates. At the far end is *informed empathy*, where our imaginative language grows out of that knowledge and becomes a way to describe both the animal's reality and our shared life before God. My goal here is not to abolish anthropomorphism, but to invite us to move from naive projection toward informed empathy.

A DOG'S KISS

Consider something as simple as a dog lick, which many dog owners will call a "kiss" and also experience as affection. However, Alexandra Horowitz, in *Inside of a Dog*, explains that licking around the mouth in canines originally cued a parent to bring up partially digested food.[1] In the wild, it was less about romance and more about dinner. She jokes that a dog might be "disappointed" when we do not respond by producing a half-eaten rabbit. What looks to us like a tender human gesture has very different roots in dog behavior.

At the same time, Horowitz notes that mouth-licking has evolved into a ritualized greeting among dogs, no longer only about food. A muzzle lick can also mean "welcome home" in the dog world. Over time, an instinctive action has become a social signal. When we call it a "kiss," we are layering a human metaphor over that signal. Technically, we are misreading the original function, but we are also trying to name the genuine connection we feel.

This is where anthropomorphism becomes both complicated and essential for the GHAB. On one hand, *naive projection* can blind us to who they really are. We may miss their actual needs or misinterpret their stress as "cuteness." On the other hand, when our language is rooted in what we actually know about a dog's body and behavior, that same imaginative language can become *informed empathy*, a way to name a holy longing for relationship and mutual delight within the GHAB.

Think of the familiar request, "Give me kisses." On the surface, it is simply a cue we teach a dog. Below, it typically reflects a unmet desire within us to be seen, loved, and welcomed. When we call a lick a "kiss," we are using a small, everyday metaphor to name that longing. We do not mean that the dog is offering a human kiss in any strict sense or that it is consciously tending to our emotional needs. Instead, we are reading a natural canine behavior as a sign of mutual affection and connection. It is not precise ethology, but it is an honest revelation of the human heart and its desire to be met through another creature.

It's here where anthropomorphism can function as a bridge between the human and animal worlds. It helps us take animals seriously as living, feeling creatures and treat them as more than objects or tools. It nudges us toward kinship and shared existence. That kinship reflects God's own vision of a reconciled creation, where wolves and lambs, children and snakes, all dwell securely in his peace (Isa. 11:6–9).

But the bridge can crack if we walk on it carelessly. Here, the *shared wound* shows itself in a subtle way. If we treat animals as though they must feel exactly what we feel, or as if they are here mainly to soothe our emotional needs, we do not close the wound between us; we put our finger on the wound and press on it. In the process, their real fears, limits, and wildness won't be seen. Similar to the fracture in Eden, where humans took from the tree and failed to listen. When we are selfish, this fracture re-appears.

In other words, when our projections replace careful attention to an animal's actual behavior and limits, the very empathy that could draw us closer becomes a tool that distances us from them. For example, a highly social dog might be kept crated for long hours each day while the humans around him repeat the phrase, "He loves his little den," pointing to his excited tail-wagging when he is finally let out, not realizing it is pent-up energy. That self-comforting story can easily drown out other signals, like pacing, whining, and excessive licking that indicate anxiety or distress. In such cases, an anthropomorphic narrative about the dog's supposed happiness does not deepen compassion; it makes it easier to ignore his actual needs, which extends the wound between us.

The invitation here is to reimagine using anthropomorphic language with humility and awareness, so it can stretch our empathy and imagination, check against what we know about animal behavior and needs, and hold it lightly, remembering that God alone fully knows the minds and hearts of both humans and animals.

At a surface level, it might seem as though nothing important is happening when we talk to our animals, and we may not immediately realize how that language influences us. The daily phrases we use, eventually, shape our imaginations. As we practice using metaphors in this way, we allow the GHAB to become more deeply ingrained in us, even through the words we say at home. We begin to see animals not as throwaway objects but as fellow creatures in God's story. Our metaphor-like commands and phrases, such as "Give me kisses," "Good girl," and "You're a good boy," become small acts of expressing God's love toward the animals in our care. In this way, *our speech becomes like a liturgy that acknowledges the Holy in everyday creaturely relationships*, gradually training our minds and habits to live more faithfully within the GHAB.

THEOLOGICAL REFLECTION ON METAPHORS RELATED TO INTERSPECIES INTERACTIONS

A TRUE STORY, A LIVING PARABLE IN FUR

One afternoon, I watched a short video of Scott, a ten-month-old kitten, and Dora, a nine-year-old Jack Russell mix, sleeping in a tangled heap. At first, they pawed at each other, exchanging playful taps and nips, but gradually Scott's head rested on Dora's side, and her breathing slowed. Dora shifted just enough to make space, then went still. Two very different creatures, with distinct instincts and histories, rested against each other as if they had always belonged together.

I could have described it as just a cute moment, but something deeper stirred in me. Their mutual trust became, in my imagination, what the Kingdom of God could look like: a peace where we expect tension, closeness where we expect distance, kindness where we might brace for teeth and claws. I found myself thinking of Isaiah's vision of wolves and lambs, calves and lions, all resting together (Isa. 11:6–9). Scott and Dora were not those animals, of course, but their *shared rest* painted a small picture of the kind of harmony God intends, in which a moment of peace softens the *shared wound* running through creation. Read theologically, their shared sleep becomes a small sign that helps us imagine the *missio Dei,* a foretaste of the peace God intends for the whole community of creation, not merely for humans (cf. Isa. 11:6–9; Col. 1:19–20). In that tangle of fur, the GHAB appears as two creatures trusting each other enough to sleep. This passage points us toward a broad horizon of reconciliation that encompasses all creation, even if it does not specify in detail how that renewal will be experienced by each creature, a shared Christian hope.

METAPHORS THAT FORM OUR IMAGINATION

Scenes like this begin to work on us as living metaphors, like a kitten tucked under a dog's chin hints that enemies might one day become neighbors. A dog lying at the feet of a child with nightmares suggests that human courage can grow in the presence of an animal's love. Or, when a former *chase* instinct becomes *rest,* we notice how the *missio Dei* is already at work re-schooling our imaginations. This dog-and-cat scene invites us to loosen our grip on fear and control and to allow relationships that let us trust, be attentive, and share vulnerability. These kinds of relationships teach us to envision God's ability to mend divisions. (cf. Col. 1:19–20; Eph. 2:14–18).[2]

METAPHORS AS MORAL FORMATION

Scripture itself is rich with animal metaphors that invite us into this way of seeing. Jesus tells his disciples, "I am sending you out like sheep among wolves. Therefore be as shrewd as serpents and as innocent as doves" (Matt. 10:16). In a single sentence, he pulls sheep, wolves, snakes, and birds into our moral vocabulary. We are not literally sheep or doves, but the comparison illuminates what it means to be vulnerable, yet wise in a broken world. Proverbs points to ants, rock badgers, locusts, and lizards as "small, yet exceedingly wise," models of diligence, dependence, and cooperation (Prov. 6:6–8; 30:24–28). Elsewhere, a dog returning to its vomit becomes a sobering picture of repeated folly (Prov. 26:11; 2 Pet. 2:22), and "ravenous wolves" warn us about false prophets who prey on the flock (Matt. 7:15; Acts 20:29). In all these cases, animal life becomes part of Scripture's moral formation, teaching us how to recognize danger, learn wisdom, and walk faithfully with God and neighbor.

GHAB, STEWARDSHIP, AND HOPE

Our shared wounds help us notice how closely our lives resemble one another in the creation and birth, in play and learning, in aging and loss. When Paul writes that "the whole creation has been groaning" (Rom. 8:22), he places that groaning inside a larger hope that creation itself will "be liberated from its bondage to decay" along with the children of God (Rom. 8:21). Seen together with the wider witness of Scripture, this shared groaning and hope invites us into practices of stewardship and compassion toward other creatures (Gen. 1:26–28; 2:15; Prov. 12:10). The GHAB becomes one of the places where we hear that groaning and learn how to join God's liberating work rather than deepen the ache, without claiming to know exactly what God's future will look like for every creature.

I have watched mother dogs after they give birth, their bodies still tired, though their spirits full of energy. They nudge each pup into place, lick them clean, and then, weeks later, bow and jump, inviting them to play. Those play bows are cute, with their front legs low and their hindquarters high and wiggling back and forth; however, they are far from frivolous; they are lessons in trust, boundaries, play, and joy.

A friend recently told me she was grieving the loss of her older dog, Jake, and recognized something similar in her other dog, CoCo. When Jake died, his little Shih Tzu companion, CoCo, kept returning to his bedding. She noticed that CoCo would go and lie down where Jake used to sleep, pressing her small body into the place that still held his scent. Nothing about that scene sounded dramatic, but it was heavy with meaning: one creature seeking nearness to another who was no longer there. CoCo's grief does not need to be identical to human grief for us to recognize that it is real. CoCo's simple act of lying on Jake's bed pulls our attention to a shared ache that runs through the GHAB.

Stories like this seem to expose the shared wound at the heart of creation. It is as if the world itself is groaning invisibly, marked by vulnerability, attachment, and loss. In that groaning, we are invited to align ourselves more fully with the cross that gives us hope and to live from a different posture. By posture, I do not mean only what we believe in our minds, but the way our whole selves lean toward God and toward the creatures around us. Posture shows up in where we place our weight, what we are ready to notice, and how quickly we move to defend ourselves or to listen.

A posture shaped by the cross makes us more open than the posture of defensiveness we may carry. Rather than standing over animals as if they exist only for our use, we begin to stand *with* them as fellow creatures, both of us held by the same Creator. Instead of rushing past their play, their fear, or their aging, we slow down enough to see their lives as part of the shared groaning Paul describes.

Practically, this posture is pausing before we speak about an animal as "just a dog" or allowing a grieving dog like CoCo to lie on an empty bed without hurrying her away. We begin to move toward compassion rather than convenience. This posture is also a way of standing under the cross with all of creation, not above it. We let the suffering of the world, human and animal, come into view without turning our faces away, and we hold that pain before God.

It needs to be said that death is not a malfunction of life to be engineered away, but a difficult part for those in the animal world because it is finite. The wound that needs healing is not mortality itself so much as the ways we deny, avoid, or harden our hearts when we face loss.

CREATION AND BIRTH

Within the narrative frame of Genesis 3, these shared beginnings unfold in a creation that now lives under a curse. Human and animal mothers alike guard fragile new life, suggesting that the wound has not erased God's original intention. Instead, it is precisely within this wounded creation that the *missio Dei* takes shape: God continues to sustain creaturely births as places where interdependence, vulnerability, and protective love are practiced and relearned across species. Each birth becomes a sign that, even in a broken world, God remains committed to sustaining and renewing life.

LIFE AND DEVELOPMENT

As life unfolds, humans and animals continue to mirror each other in remarkable ways. We all play, learn, grow, and age. We form social bonds, show affection and fear, and respond to kindness or neglect. Many animals mourn losses; many express joy when a familiar face appears.

I see these similarities as signs of God's intention that all creatures participate in the journey of becoming. They are not identical journeys, but they run alongside each other. A child learning to walk and a foal learning to stand, a teenager and a young dog testing boundaries, an older person and an aging horse moving more slowly, these moments suggest that God has interconnected growth, relationship, and change into the fabric of every life. Even after the fall, humans and animals still carry this design, striving to navigate a world that is not as it should be. I often think about the times I have taken my dog to visit elderly residents at a nursing home and watched them reach for the leash of a gray-muzzled therapy dog. Both of them move slowly and carefully, joints stiff and steps slower than before, but they both brighten at the sight of a different face. The wrinkled hands resting on the worn fur become a small picture of how aging is common ground across species.

DEATH AND AFTERLIFE

Death is a universal experience shared by all living beings. People die. Animals die. Fields lie fallow, and forests burn, yet new life always begins again. Different traditions describe the afterlife in various ways, and Christians continue to wrestle with what God's future holds for animals. Still, Scripture clearly states that God notices every sparrow that falls (Matt. 10:29).

Psi's death made this real for me. By then, she was fifteen. Her body had thinned; her steps had become uncertain and staggered. We had taken her to the veterinarian, tried medications and injections to ease her pain and support her joints, but she had reached a point where death was touching her more than life. On the day she died, she simply lay down in her crate at home and did not get up again, while customers arrived to drop off their dogs for boarding in the driveway. A neighbor came over to help us dig her grave in the back field. Jenny and our neighbor dug while I stayed inside to receive a client's dog. As soon as their dog was safely settled, I walked out to her graveside because I loved her and needed to see that she was cared for even at the very end. They had wrapped her in the blanket she had slept on for years and lowered her into the ground near the place where she once ran and barked. There were no trumpets or visions, only dirt under our nails, tears we could not quite hold back, and a simple but heartfelt prayer to give thanks for her life.

Naming this shared mortality does not aim to erase the uniqueness of humans or animals, but to deepen our humility and compassion. When we remember that animals, like us, are finite and vulnerable, our sense of responsibility toward them can grow. The GHAB is not only about comfort and companionship; it is also about honoring the lives of creatures who are as fragile and dependent on God's mercy as we are, trusting that the God who sees every sparrow's fall also sees theirs, and ours (Matt. 10:29; Rom. 8:19–22).

Christians have long differed over what God's future holds for animals. In this book, I'm speaking of a hopeful trust in God's care for all creatures, not a settled dogma about how animal afterlife must work.

EMBODIED METAPHORS: FALLING, SLEEPING, GROWING

Beyond life stages, everyday experiences function as embodied metaphors, actual events that point beyond themselves. Falling, sleeping, seeing, growing, illness, and death are not "just images"; they are realities shared by humans and animals, often holding spiritual meaning.

Pastors and spiritual directors sometimes see themselves as "walking wounded" who become "wounded healers," borrowing Henri Nouwen's image in *The Wounded Healer*.[3] The phrase resonates with us because it comes from real experience: people who have been hurt and, through grace, can walk alongside others in their pain. I recognize myself in that description. We relate similarly when we see a limping dog comfort a grieving child or an aging horse patiently carry a nervous rider. Their vulnerability does not erase their strength; it becomes part of how they care.

We also often use animal idioms unconsciously, like "birds of a feather flock together," "busy as a bee," "eager beaver," and "lone wolf." These sayings reflect how closely we observe other creatures and how we borrow their patterns to describe ourselves. They demonstrate that human and animal lives are already interconnected in our speech, even when our theology falls behind.

Metaphors can certainly be misused and obscure more than they reveal. But when they arise from real, shared experiences, between God, humans, and animals, they can help us name complex or mysterious truths, such as "seeing" God's fingerprints in creation or recognizing our own wounds in the eyes of a suffering creature.

Not all human–animal stories are warm and lovely. Some are marked by hardship, fear, and loss. In the next section, you will read stories of suffering that become places where God can still bring spiritual renewal and growth, even when the shared wound is most visible.

In all of this, we begin to see that our wound is not only personal or private; it is inter-generational and cross-species. Genesis 3, our own stories of harm and protection, and even the phrases we use every day, all reveal how deeply connected we are to the animals and places that share our lives. The GHAB can be marked by fear, loss, and misunderstanding, as well as by fierce loyalty and unexpected certainty.

Naming our shared wound is not meant to leave us stuck in shame; it is the first step toward living differently. In Christ, we are invited into a story that resists old patterns of domination and indifference and learns new ways of seeing, speaking, and acting with love. That is where we turn next, *A Shared Distance*, tracing how this wound continues to shape our separations from animals and creation, and how God begins to heal those distances.

QUESTIONS FOR REFLECTION AND PRACTICE

» Which story or image in this chapter most clearly reflects a shared wound in your own life with animals or creation: Genesis 3's deep wound, the dog and the shoes, Psi and Paris as "guardians of the night," Harry the mouse in Kuwait, Winston needing a break, CoCo's grief? What does that moment reveal to you about both the harm and the hope that run through the GHAB?

» This week, choose *one* way to live from a "posture shaped by the cross" toward an animal or a place: pausing before dismissing an animal as "just a dog," allowing a grieving animal to linger in its own way, or adjusting your language so it better reflects an animal's real needs and limits. Afterwards, ask: how did that intentional posture change what you noticed, how you felt, or your relationship with that creature or place?

NOTES

1. Alexandra Horowitz, *Inside of a Dog: What Dogs See, Smell, and Know* (New York: Scribner, 2010), 50-51.
2. It is not a claim that animals forgive one another in the same conscious way that humans do. Rather, this language points to the way God's reconciling life upholds and renews the entire community of creation.
3. Henri J. M. Nouwen, *The Wounded Healer: Ministry in Contemporary Society* (New York: Image Books, 1979), 88.

9

A SHARED DISTANCE

The mission-driven impact of our spiritual calling to work alongside God in his creation has historically encountered barriers. I'm not simply listing the mistakes we have made, but discerning the wounds that have made it more difficult for us to experience creation as an analogous sign of grace. These barriers, deeply rooted in Christian history, have shaped how followers of Christ relate to the natural world. Theologian and Old Testament scholar Ellen Davis observes that misreading Scripture's agrarian vision has often led us to view the land as a commodity rather than a covenantal partner in God's purposes.[1] Seeing these influences can help us understand why reclaiming a creation-honoring spirituality is so important today. What follows is not a full history lesson but a kind of confession, in which we can examine the habits and ideas that have shaped our thoughts and led us to forget that the earth and its creatures are our neighbors in God's mission. They are participants within the GHAB, though I must say that animals or landscapes do not mediate salvation in the same way Christ does (1 Tim. 2:5).

DOMINION MISINTERPRETED: STEWARDSHIP VERSUS EXPLOITATION

One significant historical barrier has been the misinterpretation of the biblical doctrine of dominion in Genesis 1:26–28. When read alongside God's charge to "till and keep" the garden (Gen. 2:15), dominion is not domination but a form of *priestly* caretaking. The verbs used there, *'ābad* ("to till/serve") and *šāmar* ("to keep/guard"),[2] are later used for the ministry of priests who "serve" and "keep" the sanctuary, suggesting that Adam's vocation is to tend the garden as a kind of temple, on behalf of God and for the sake of all who dwell there (Num. 3:7–8). In that sense, human dominion is intended as a liturgical service that protects and nurtures life rather than as raw power that seizes and consumes it.[3] Similarly, the shepherd imagery that runs through Scripture suggests attentive care, guidance, and self-sacrificial protection (Ps. 23; Jn. 10:11), so to say humans are given dominion is to say they are called to be the shepherds of creation. Instead of viewing dominion as a call for stewardship, shepherding, and care, it has sometimes been interpreted as a license to exploit and control creation, bending it to human will. This misreading of Genesis has justified environmental degradation and the subjugation of animals, rather than inspiring a mindset of priestly shepherding. In GHAB terms, part of what it means to live out our priestly vocation is to tend the shared world we inhabit with other creatures.

THE AUGUSTINIAN LEGACY: DUALISM AND COMPLEXITY

A second obstacle stems from Augustine's legacy. Augustine becomes a figure of tension rather than a villain, and in many ways, I see my own story reflected in that tension. Since I became a new creation in Christ, I have followed the Lord's call, but when I expressed that calling within certain denominations, it was not always accepted or supported because I'm female. I have continued to follow Christ without regret, yet these experiences reveal how deeply some faith communities still live with their own dualisms and divisions. When we learn to rank spirit over body or heaven over earth, it can become easier, often without realizing it, to rank some bodies and voices over others, including men over women. Augustine's writings often emphasized a duality between the spiritual and material realms, encouraging Christians to prioritize the soul over the body and heaven over earth. This has contributed to a tendency in Western Christianity to view the material world, including nature and the body, as distractions or even barriers to true communion with God. As a result, encountering God in creation or experiencing the sacred through animals and the environment was often viewed with suspicion, as if the GHAB were at best an emotional concept and at worst spiritually dangerous.

In a similar way, Augustine's own spiritual life was more complex than this trend suggests. In his *Confessions*, he describes moments of profound connection with God through beauty, poetry, and song: "What utterances I used to send up to Thee in those Psalms and how was I inflamed toward Thee by them."[4] Although his theology often leaned toward dualism, he found comfort and spiritual renewal through prayer inspired by creation. Augustine's tension reminds us that if our doctrines distance us from creation, experience can still draw us back to the sacredness God instilled in all that exists. Alongside Augustinian influence, other voices also emerged, such as the Benedictine abbess, writer, and poet Hildegard of Bingen, and Francis of Assisi, who refused to dismiss creation as a distraction and instead chose to celebrate the earth as a living hymn sung to the Creator. These witnesses suggest that the GHAB was never fully silenced; it *continued singing* beneath the surface of our theology, *waiting to be heard.*

INDUSTRIALIZATION AND DISCONNECTION FROM CREATION

Further separation occurred with the Industrial Revolution, which started in the late eighteenth century and continued into the nineteenth and early twentieth centuries, significantly changing human relationships with land and animals. As factories grew and cities expanded, many people moved from farms and villages into cities, exchanging the daily work of tending soil and livestock for life in offices, shops, and factories. Creation was more and more seen as raw material for making profit, rather than as a community of fellow beings to be carefully shepherded. Historian Lynn White Jr. argued that "certain strands of Western Christian thought helped underwrite this ecological crisis by encouraging a posture of mastery over nature rather than companionship with it."[5] His essay has served more as a spark for debate than as a final verdict. Other historians remind us that the roots of our crisis are multi-layered: Carolyn Merchant, for example, traces how the rise of a mechanistic worldview in early modern Europe, when treating nature as a machine rather than a living community, helped justify exploitation, while Clarence Glacken shows that strong forms of anthropocentrism were already present in classical Greek thought long before Christianity.[6] Even so, White's warning remains important: theology can either bless or resist exploitative habits.

I see how easily our disconnection from creation, namely animals, seeps into our personal lives, shaping the way we invalidate their worth, when instead we are invited to receive them as partners in God's healing work. As an Animal-Assisted Activity (AAA), when a patient has petted Winston, the encounter opened doors in the human heart that my words alone could not touch; yet the same people may sometimes speak of him as *nothing* more *than* a donkey. Those simple words felt like a betrayal of how deeply we have been shaped by the idea that animals are tools for our comfort rather than catalysts who might help mend relationships in a broken world. In my work with Winston, I try to follow best practices during an AAA by prioritizing his consent and well-being, monitoring his stress signals, and ending or redirecting visits when he shows he has had enough.

In those moments, I can feel the GHAB constrict: a living bond reduced to a test of usefulness.

This shift did more than change economies; it reshaped imaginations. When most of life occurs on pavement and under bright lights, it becomes harder to recognize ourselves as *creatures among creatures* and easier to imagine ourselves as primarily managers of resources. In missional terms, that disconnection is more likely to weaken our capacity to discern God's presence in the ordinary gifts of land, water, and animal life. If we rarely touch the soil or notice the lives that depend on it, we may begin to struggle to believe that God might meet us while we are visiting with an animal. Reclaiming a creation-honoring spirituality, then, is *not* nostalgia for a simpler time; it is a way of recovering our vocation within the *missio Dei,* and of re-opening our hearts to the GHAB as a place where that vocation is learned.

LEARNING TO SEE BEYOND THE SCREEN

Another significant barrier, and possibly the greatest in our time, is the rise of technology, which can further distance us from experiencing animals as instruments of God's love. This technological divide fosters a form of "ecological dualism," a way of living as if our real lives happen on screens and in abstract spaces while the soil, water, and fellow creatures that sustain us fade into the background.

We are living in what is often called the Information Age, a time when nearly everything we might want to know sits at our fingertips. It is easy to become consumed with gathering data, scrolling social media, and searching for answers about God online, even as our bodies sit still and our senses grow dull.

Yet I believe this information saturation is preparing the ground for a deeper hunger. Over time, some seekers will grow weary of second and third-hand knowledge of God and begin to long for lived, embodied encounters with God in creation. Instead of overwhelming themselves with endless opinions, arguments, clickbait, and "likes," they will step outside in search of thin places, where their questions about God and suffering can be carried into the presence of trees, rivers, and animals who simply are what God made them to be and who, in their own way, become teachers of God's wisdom (Job 12:7–10). So, the future of spirituality may look less like defending arguments on a screen and more like entering immersive experiences in the more-than-human world, where the GHAB becomes a shared atmosphere of breath, touch, and presence.

One response to ecological dualism invites us to re-orient our digital habits toward practices that reunite soul and soil. For example, a person whose days are filled with texts, emails, and online news might choose to set aside one evening each week as a brief sabbath from screens. I once came across an eye-opening phrase, whose original source is long forgotten: "scrolling is the new smoking." I have never smoked, but the comparison makes sense to me; both are easy, addictive habits we turn to for comfort or escape. Instead of scrolling, we might take a slow walk with our dog, spend time with a cat, or visit a neighbor's pet, bringing our questions and grief into that shared breathing space. In the stillness of listening to a horse's steady breath or feeling a dog's warm weight against our leg, we might discover that God's presence is not an argument to be won online but a tenderness encountered in the company of another creature. Such practices do not reject technology outright but situate it within a larger, more embodied way of being, in which animals and the land become *companions* and *co-pilgrims* in our search for God. Each of these small choices becomes a way to step back into the GHAB intentionally *rather than* by accident.

Modern life is full of other dualisms that shape our behavior: the separation between work and rest can erode our sense of Sabbath; the divide between urban and rural spaces can lead us to forget our dependence on land and animals; and digital tensions can draw us away from embodied spiritual experiences. Even within ourselves, intellect may trump emotion, or spirit may overshadow body, thereby neglecting God's design for us as whole, integrated beings.

Yet Genesis 1:26 calls us to a different place: to respect animal habitats, practice stewardship of creation, and shepherd animals as central to our original vocation. Bridging these dualisms by reconnecting with the natural world, honoring its rhythms, and embracing our role as caretakers is essential to faithfully living out the *missio Dei* and to embracing the GHAB as a gift.

THE SPIRITUAL CALL: TRANSFORMATION OF THE NOT-YET-HOLY

The call to live as followers of Christ is rooted in the biblical witness that all things belong to God and that creation itself is ordered toward God's holiness (Lev. 11:44–45; Rom. 11:36). Some realities already participate more visibly in that holiness; others, in a sense, remain not yet transparent to it. To put it differently, a neighbor who feeds those who are hungry may reflect God's holiness more clearly than a system that profits from their hunger, even though God's presence is at work in both. We can, therefore, speak cautiously of the Holy and the not-yet-holy. These are not permanent labels of worth or a way of sorting the world into good and bad. Instead, they name the difference between realities that already bear some visible likeness to God's love and those in which that likeness is resisted or obscured. Every life, place, and relationship is capable, by grace, of being drawn more deeply into God's sanctifying presence, sharing more fully in Christ's holiness (Heb. 10:10; 1 Thess. 5:23–24). How we treat people, animals, and the environment can either overshadow or cooperate with that intention. The missional task of God's people is to join, however imperfectly, in this work of grace by continually offering the not-yet-holy back to God, including the parts of the GHAB we have ignored, misused, or left unnamed.

In the strict sense, only God makes anything holy; holiness belongs to God alone (Isa. 6:3). Yet Christians have long asked what it means to participate in that holiness and whether, in Christ and empowered through the Spirit, our actions can become instruments of God's sanctifying work. Some argue that only God can sanctify and that human actions, no matter how well-intentioned, always fall short of that divine act. Others emphasize that, in Christ and through the Spirit, we are invited to "share in his holiness" (Heb. 12:10) so that when we show up with open hearts and faithful presence, God, whose very life is holy love, may work through us as vessels, allowing his holiness to become more clearly manifest in our actions, relationships, and spaces. Whatever our position in that debate, what is clear is that any visible holiness in the world is first and last God's work, in which we are graciously allowed to participate.

Importantly, this is never a journey of our own achievement but a participation in God's holiness. The transformation of the not-yet-holy does not arise from human effort or optimism; it depends entirely on the One who alone is Holy and who, by the Spirit, draws creation toward communion with himself (2 Pet. 1:4).

WHERE SHARED DISTANCE BEGINS TO THIN

God's breadth and love extend to all creatures; His life-giving presence sustains all living things, even as He dwells in a distinctive way with His people and the saints. As Jürgen Moltmann, a leading twentieth-century theologian known for his work on hope and the Spirit, describes God's "immanent transcendence" (God's presence is everywhere), echoing the Holy Spirit as the *fons vitae*, the fountain of life.[7] In other words, God's life-giving presence is not limited to sacred times and places but permeates every moment of existence. As Moltmann argues, every experience of life can become a discovery of this living source of the Spirit's power.[8] For Christians, God's presence in all things is known most clearly through the crucified and risen Christ, whose cross stands at the center of God's reconciling work for creation.

God's living presence can meet us in every experience, and then those encounters, especially in the company of other creatures, become the raw material for the stories through which we bear witness to His work. Many of those stories, if we name them honestly, are GHAB stories; they are episodes in which God, a human, and another creature share *a single thread of grace*.

Our purpose on earth includes "telling all his wonderful acts" (1 Chron. 16:9), a liturgy that extends beyond formal worship and into the stories we share. Whether or not we explicitly mention animals or landscapes, it is our duty to witness to God's work. In modern spirituality influenced by Celtic Christian themes, these moments are often called "thin places," where heaven and earth seem to meet and God's Spirit connects creation and humanity, drawing us back to the God revealed most fully in Jesus Christ. As Hicks, Valentine, and Wilson affirm, "The goal of a Christ-centered life does not happen apart from the rest of God's creation," and "Glorifying God is a vocation we share with all creation."[9] To speak of the GHAB, then, is simply to notice how that shared space often takes on flesh in our relationships.

WHERE DISTANCE BEGINS TO THIN

One autumn afternoon, after a morning spent answering texts, reading emails, and scrolling through news on my phone, I realized I had not stepped outside all day. The sky beyond the window was a flat, gray, cloudy backdrop. It seemed more like an invitation than a backdrop for my place in the world. Out of habit, I reached for my phone again, then stopped and set it on the table instead. Winston was standing at the fence, his ears tilted forward, watching the road as if he were waiting for someone.

I pulled on my boots and walked out to him. The air smelled faintly of rain and hay. When I reached the gate, Winston walked over and lowered his head so that his muzzle rested against my chest. For a few long breaths, neither of us moved. I could feel the roughness of his whiskers through my shirt, the warmth of his breath, the steady rise and fall of his neck under my hand. No alerts or notifications were issued, yet something essential was taking place. A long-eared friend and a tired human stood together in the damp pasture, saying nothing, and somehow the distance I had been feeling, from my own body, from God, from the world, began to thin.

Nothing dramatic happened. There were no visions or audible words, only the sense that I was being *re-placed*: back on the earth, beside a fellow creature. The afternoon was still full of unfinished work, unanswered text messages, and the same unresolved questions about suffering and hope. But for a moment, my life felt less like a set of problems and more like a shared story unfolding.

Later, when I tried to describe that moment in my journal, I realized how easily I could have missed it. I could have stayed at my desk, scrolling past more opinions *about* God instead of stepping into a thin place where God's life-giving presence was already waiting for us. Winston and I did not solve the world's crises that day, but our simple standing together became, for me, a hidden act of transforming the not-yet-holy. A screen-saturated, distracted afternoon was offered back to God and, in the company of a patient donkey, began to be re-ordered towards a shared moment and mindfulness. In language from earlier chapters, that afternoon was a lived glimpse of the GHAB: God's nearness felt through a woman and a donkey in a muddy field.

That is the kind of transformation this chapter has been aiming for. Thin places, where our distance from God, from animals, and from our own bodies begins to soften, can become spaces where God's holiness encounters our not-yet-holy habits, and where new stories emerge. As we learn to notice and share those stories, we do not avoid the wounds of our shared distance, but we start, when we are faithful to simple practices, to live as if animals are once again our neighbors in the *missio Dei*, as if the GHAB were not an exception to discipleship but one of its common classrooms.

QUESTIONS FOR REFLECTION AND PRACTICE

- As you think about the barriers mentioned in this chapter, where do you most recognize "shared distance" in your own life with animals and creation? Is it in how you speak about animals, how often you touch the land, or how much of your day is spent away from the other-than-human world?
- This week, choose *one* small practice that helps "thin" that distance: for example, a brief sabbath from screens to take a slow walk with an animal, pausing before you call an animal "just" or "only" something, or noticing one thin place (your job, a park, or a pasture) where you can stand quietly with a creature before God. Afterwards, ask: how did that simple act of *intention* change my sense of God's presence, of myself, and of this animal or place as my neighbor in the *missio Dei*, and as part of the GHAB?

NOTES

1. Ellen F. Davis, *Scripture, Culture, and Agriculture: An Agrarian Reading of the Bible* (Cambridge: Cambridge University Press, 2009), 7.
2. For *ābad* and *šāmar* as priestly terms, see Gordon J. Wenham, *Word Biblical Commentary: Genesis 1–15* (Waco, TX: Word Books, 1987), 67–68. John H. Walton, *The Lost World of Adam and Eve: Genesis 2–3 and the Human Origins Debate* (Downers Grove, IL: IVP Academic, 2015), 82–84.
3. For further reading on "dominion" as *priestly/servant rule*, see Ellen F. Davis, *Scripture, Culture, and Agriculture: An Agrarian Reading of the Bible* (Cambridge: Cambridge University Press, 2009), 29–30.
4. Augustine, *Confessions*, trans. Henry Chadwick (Oxford: Oxford University Press, 1991), 9.4.8.

5. Lynn White Jr., "The Historical Roots of Our Ecologic Crisis," *Science* 155, no. 3767 (1967): 1203–7; Carolyn Merchant, *The Death of Nature: Women, Ecology, and the Scientific Revolution* (San Francisco: Harper & Row, 1980).
6. Clarence J. Glacken, *Traces on the Rhodian Shore: Nature and Culture in Western Thought from Ancient Times to the End of the Eighteenth Century* (Berkeley: University of California Press, 1967).
7. Jürgen Moltmann, *The Spirit of Life: A Universal Affirmation*, trans. Margaret Kohl (Minneapolis: Fortress Press, 1992), Kindle ed., loc. 1393.
8. Moltmann, *The Spirit of Life*, Kindle loc. 1182.
9. John Mark Hicks, Bobby Valentine, and Mark Wilson, *Embracing Creation: God's Forgotten Mission* (Abilene, TX: Leafwood Publishers, 2016), Kindle ed., loc. 542–44.

10

A SHARED HOPE

In the last chapter, we lingered with *thin places* and named some of the ways we pull back: keeping animals at arm's length when they are inconvenient and insulating ourselves from their suffering. Those distances are not harmless; they grow out of the same deep fracture that runs through our relationships with God, one another, animals, and the earth. They also dull our awareness of the GHAB, as if that shared life between us were optional rather than part of how God meets us.

We have already seen that fracture in Scripture and in our own lives. Genesis 3 tells the story of a shared rupture rather than a private mistake: a serpent, two humans, trees, the ground, and God are all drawn into a single scene and touched by the same wound. We traced that wound into ordinary places, and along the way, we noticed how our language reveals how deeply our lives are already intertwined with the animals we share our days with. Even when we don't explicitly name it, the GHAB hovers at the edges of our days, like *a thin place* waiting to be seen.

Naming these distances and this shared wound is important, but it is not the end of the story. In Christ, we are invited into a different story. Jesus' story resists old patterns of domination, dispossession, and indifference, and it gradually teaches us new ways of seeing, speaking, and acting with love. *A Shared Hope* does not deny the fracture; it begins by telling the truth about it. But it also asks the next, daring question: *What might it look like, within this bond between God, humans, and animals, to live as if reconciliation were already underway?*

What follows in this chapter is not a blueprint for perfection, but a collection of experiences and practices through which reimagined stories begin to emerge, old scripts are interrupted, new habits are formed, and the GHAB is renewed. These are not abstract ideals; they are small vignettes of what life can look like when we treat the GHAB as a place of discipleship and hope.

TURNING FROM OLD SCRIPTS

In a world shaped by Genesis 3, it's entirely natural to live out unexamined scripts without even realizing it. One script suggests that animals exist mainly for our convenience or comfort. If they please us, they may stay; if they annoy, frighten, or cost us money, they can be ignored, rehomed, or removed. There are other views in which creation is considered background scenery for human drama: a stage set we can rearrange or discard. These patterns are so ingrained that we often do not recognize them as part of the wound. They appear in subtle ways:

» The spider in the bathtub was washed down the drain without a second thought.
» The stray cat is shooed away with a kick of the foot.
» The aging dog is left mostly alone because its slowness interrupts our pace.
» The fields around us are paved over without a second thought.

These choices are not as drastic as Genesis 3, yet each one participates in the same broken web of relationships. When we treat animals and places as disposable, we rehearse the lie that our lives are not deeply connected, that what happens to other creatures does not really matter to God or to us. We shrink the GHAB down to a private feeling instead of a real, shared life. A *different story* begins when we allow the Spirit to interrupt these scripts and create a new pattern (of being and doing). It does not require us to rescue every animal or solve every environmental crisis. Instead, it invites us to pay attention, to pause before we act, and to ask a different set of questions: *What is really happening here? How might love look in this moment? What story do I want to live with this creature and this part of creation?*

MODEST ACTS AND DIFFERENT STORIES

Our stories that are a bit different rarely begin with grand gestures. More often, they start with the small choices we make.

Sometimes it looks like sparing a spider and carrying it outside rather than crushing it with a shoe. The act takes thirty seconds, but it tells a *different story*, one of being thoughtful and about whose life matters and who belongs in God's world.

Sometimes it means pausing when a stray cat appears at the edge of the yard. Instead of seeing a nuisance, we might see a hungry neighbor. We still cannot do everything, but perhaps we can offer a dish of food, make a phone call to a shelter, or at least refuse to add more fear to its already anxious life.

Sometimes the *different story* involves a new way of living with the other, even if temporarily, yet as simple as lingering with an aging dog. We choose to walk more slowly, to adjust our plans, to make room for the creature who once adjusted to us. In doing so, we resist a culture that prizes usefulness and speed above all else. We say with our time, "You still matter. You are not just a memory of your younger self. You are a fellow creature under God's care, and I will not discard you because you have grown old."

None of these acts will make headlines; yet each one can become a form of repentance, a small turning away from the old patterns of Genesis 3 and toward the reconciling work of Christ. They are mustard-seed moments in the GHAB, tiny shifts in how God, a human, and another creature share existence.

REPENTANCE, RENEWAL, AND THE GHAB

The language of repentance can feel heavy, but at its heart, repentance is simply a change of direction, the Spirit-prompted decision to walk a different way. In the context of the GHAB, it sounds like this: I used to ignore the seemingly insignificant lives around me; *now I want to notice them.* I used to see animals only as tools, ornaments, or background; *now I choose to see them as fellow creatures in God's story.* I used to assume creation would just yield to my demands; *now I want to ask what it means to care for the places that care for me.*

When we take even one step in this direction, we participate in God's renewing work within the GHAB. Our choices will still be imperfect, and we will not always agree on how to show mercy in difficult situations, but it is not about getting everything right; however, it is about letting Christ reshape our default settings from harm toward healing and from indifference to attentive love. As the Apostle Paul writes, all creation is groaning, waiting for the revealing of the children of God (Rom. 8:19–22). Can we accept that part of the revealing may be very ordinary, like refilling a dog's water bowl with fresh water or slowing down to let a squirrel cross the road? These are not "extra" to our faith; they are ways the GHAB becomes *a site of conversion.*

OUR KINGDOM-SHAPED STORIES

You likely already carry your own *alternative stories*, moments when you felt nudged to act differently toward an animal or a place:

» a time you chose to adopt rather than buy,
» a decision to stay with a sick pet longer than was convenient,
» a choice to protect a patch of land or a nest of birds others saw as expendable,
» a habit of blessing animals you pass on a walk, even if you never know their names.

These may seem too diminutive to mention, but they are not trivial to God. They are signs that the shared wound is not the final word, glimpses of the Kingdom breaking in through the GHAB.

As you continue reading, I invite you to name these stories, perhaps even write them down. Share them with a friend, a spiritual director, or a study group. Ask together: *What is God teaching us through these encounters? How might we live even more faithfully within this bond?*

A shared *different story* can be one of redemption, which does not erase the wound, but it opens a path through it. On that path, surrounded by creatures great and small, we may begin to sense the healed creation God is even now bringing to life.

THE KINGDOM OF GOD

The different stories we begin to live with animals and places are foretastes of an eternal story, the Kingdom of God. As Jesus said, "The kingdom of heaven is like a mustard seed, which a man took and planted in his field.

Though it is the smallest of all seeds, yet when it grows, it is the largest of garden plants and becomes a tree, so that the birds come and perch in its branches" (Matt. 13:31–32).

As a contemplative Christian, I'm drawn to the work of love and unity among people and creation. I have shared spaces of silence, lament, and hope with people from many different backgrounds, including those who do not share my Christian faith. In those settings, my own worship remains centered on the Triune God fully revealed in Christ, even as I listen for how God may be at work in others' lives. All creation can enter into spaces of shared silence, prayer, lament, and hope, trusting that the Holy One, fully revealed in Christ, will never be contained by our language or traditions and is at work in ways that surpass our understanding (Phil. 4:7).

I also believe that God's truth and presence can be discerned across many paths and traditions. We are invited into a unity rooted not in sameness of belief but in a shared turning toward Love, as Christians understand it in Christ. For me, this unity begins with the call to love God and to love our neighbors, human and animal alike. As John writes, "Whoever does not love does not know God, because God is love" (1 Jn. 4:8). Love is not *merely* a moral virtue; it is a *reflection* of who God is, the bridge across individual, religious, and even species differences. The GHAB can serve as a bridge connecting the triad of God, humans, and animals.

THE KINGDOM'S CREATURELY KOINONIA

Creation itself provides a living parable of this shared Kingdom: each creature has its own role, yet all work together to keep life going, a kind of *cyclical creaturely koinonia*, a circle in which life is received, shared, and given back again.

Pollinators such as bees and butterflies serve as agents of life, carrying pollen between blossoms so that fruits, vegetables, and flowers can abound. Predators such as lions and eagles keep prey populations in check, preventing imbalance. Decomposers such as fungi, earthworms, and microbes break down what has died, returning nutrients to the soil so that new life can grow. Herbivores shape plant communities through their grazing. Even while hummingbirds depend on particular flowers, they, in turn, help those plants flourish. Others take on broad tasks like the scavengers that consume what is left behind, cleansing and recycling organic matter that other animals cannot use. All are needed. Together they form a body in which each member's contribution is distinct and vital, much like the Body of Christ that Paul describes in 1 Corinthians 12.

Seen through the lens of the GHAB, this living body of creation reminds us that the Kingdom of God is not only about human souls. It is about the renewal of a whole community of life, embraced by God's wisdom and sustained by His love. The creaturely *koinonia* we see now, like this fragile, interdependent fellowship of pollinators, predators, and scavengers, in which life is sustained through these patterns, will need to be healed, offering only a partial sign of the Kingdom to come. It is not a perfect mirror of God's final peace but a partial sign of the Kingdom to come, a reminder of how deeply all our lives are already connected. It is like a symbol that points toward the day when "creation itself will be set free" (Rom. 8:21), and every creature will take its place in God's reconciled world (Rev. 5:13).

So far, we've explored the GHAB through theology, Scripture, and various stories. Now I want to slow down and look at just one small circle in the larger *koinonia*: my years with Beau and how our bond continues to shape my life. It's in this bond between one person and one dog that these themes come into sharp focus for me, which was a providential sign of the Kingdom we have been exploring. Beau's story of loyalty built over time is a close-up photograph of the GHAB.

PROVIDENCE: WHEN GOD SENDS A HOUND

My application to adopt a dog had been sitting with a rescue for months when I first started seeing Beau trot through our fields, ribs showing, head hanging low, too scared to let me near. I felt a knot of sadness watching him, but also an irritation I didn't want to admit. I already had enough on my plate and did*n't* want to fall in love with a needy, half-wild hound. When he finally let me feed him, there was no magic moment or instant bond. I felt awkward and guarded, and I didn't click with him as I did with my other dogs. About a week after Beau found me, the adoption agency called to say they were ready to place a dog. I glanced over at Beau and told them I wasn't interested. When I hung up, a wave of guilt and confusion washed over me. Something in me was resisting a gift I didn't yet understand.

Looking back, I realize how badly I misjudged him.

At first, I wrote off this stray dog that had been watching our house for a long time. I knew it was a hound breed because I grew up around hounds, and I remember the old farm talk: hounds were noisy, stubborn, and meant for hunting, not much else. I carried a bowl of food to the end of our driveway and set it down. He wouldn't come close to eat, so I picked up the bowl and started walking home. He followed me all the way to the back porch, where I set it down again. As I watched his long ears and anxious eyes as he ate from the bowl, the old farm talk and prejudice kicked in before I even realized it. I fed him because he was hungry, but I didn't expect much more until I found the number on his collar.

When I called, his previous owner told me they had adopted him from a shelter during a divorce. The husband was supposed to take Beau to a nearby farm, but that never happened, and by the time I called, they were ready to give him away. Later that day, they sent me a photo of "Cylus," now named Beau, cable-tied to a doghouse, looking as if his spirit had been chained along with him. My earlier indifference felt like a wound added to his others, and the image broke my heart. I suddenly saw not a "dumb hound" but a dog who had been passed around, restrained, and misunderstood. I could not ignore that his story touched an old ache in me; as a child and even as an adult, I often felt passed around and unwanted.

In that moment, I began to sense that God had intentionally placed Beau in my life. Unbeknownst to me at the time, he was not just a stray on my porch, but an unexpected way the Kingdom of God was breaking into my heart. What looked like a coincidence was, in the GHAB language, a divine introduction: God using a hound to walk me into a new way of seeing.

LEARNING TO TRUST ONE ANOTHER

At first, our bond was a bit rough around the edges, and Beau stayed on the yard's perimeter, watching and unsure. He would play with visiting dogs but kept his emotional distance from me. I was unfamiliar with an independent, aloof hound who didn't stick to me like glue, unlike my previous dogs. I felt like I had a lot to learn, and so did Beau, but over time, we began to learn from each other.

A turning point happened on an ordinary evening. I was sitting on the back steps when Beau chose, without being coaxed, to lie down beside me; it wasn't at my feet, not across the yard, but right beside me. He didn't look up or lick my hand. He simply rested his body against my leg and sighed. It was in that shared breath that something shifted. I felt a trust that hadn't been there before, and with it, a hint that God was working through this unlikely friend.

Over time, the space between us slowly closed. Beau became a life-changing companion, and the early awkwardness gave way to a strong, steady bond built through countless walks and adventures.

Together, we participated in various dog sports: Rally, Obedience, Trick Dog, and especially Scent Work, where Beau's talents truly shone. Our time in the ring stood as a testament to trust, teamwork, and shared joy. Through Beau, I learned an invaluable lesson: *do not* judge a dog by appearances. The "dumb hound" I once dismissed turned out to be the most intelligent dog I have ever known.

Beyond the competitions, Beau's presence filled the house with little joys like the thump of his tail against the wall, his goofy play bows in the kitchen, and the weight of his head on my knee when I prayed. He filled our days with comfort and friendship, and also with a kind of laughter I especially needed in that season of my life.

Ultimately, my relationship with Beau has shown the transformative power of love and the importance of accepting the gifts God gives us, no matter how unexpected. What started as confusion and sadness became, over time, a *God-wink,* a message that God was saying, "I'm here, reshaping how you see and love."[1] The GHAB, in our case, was not an idea in a textbook, but a brown-and-white hound who slept by my bed and waited at the door.

BEAU'S GIFT: SCENT WORK

The American Kennel Club (AKC) features a sport called Scent Work, a dog activity that, through training, transforms a dog's natural love of sniffing into a structured game. Dogs search for hidden scents and indicate when they've found the source. Handlers are there to keep them safe and interpret their body language, but the actual work belongs to the dog. For shy or reserved dogs, Scent Work can boost confidence and happiness; for dogs like Beau, it becomes a way to shine. When I first entered a search area with Beau, I was still learning to trust him. The space could be a simple room, a row of vehicles, or a corner of a field. Somewhere in that area, a cotton swab infused with birch, anise, clove, or cypress oil was hidden out of sight. I would unclip Beau's leash, give him the signal to search, and watch.

He would bound forward, ears flopping, nose immediately catching invisible threads of scent. His playful bounce turned purposeful as he zigzagged through the space, stirring up the air like a mini tornado. Then, as he closed in on the source, his body changed: his movement slowed, his head lowered, his tail stilled with a little tremble on the tip. Finally, he would sit or paw at the exact spot where the scent was most potent and look back at me, eyes shining, as if to say, *Here. I've found it!*

My job in that moment was simple: trust him. I would raise my hand and call, "Alert!" to the judge. Over and over again, Beau was right.

Standing beside him in those moments, I felt a kind of wonder that words barely describe. Beau, once dismissed as a dumb and dirty stray, was now guiding me with a sense far keener than my own. His nose could detect what I could not see or smell. Our roles reversed: I was no longer the one in control; I was the one learning to follow.

Although Beau has passed, he left me with lasting memories of those searches and etched valuable lessons into my heart: do not crowd the dog; do not rush to call an alert; prioritize safety when heat or stress rises; and remember that anxiety can run down the leash. Most of all, ribbons or titles are not the goal but the joy of the game and the bond you share.

My experiences with Beau eventually led me to become an AKC Scent Work judge. That role required more study to understand wind, temperature, humidity, and how scent moves through different spaces. But beneath all the technical details was something simpler: a continued sense of awe at what God has placed inside these animals and at how that gift can draw humans and dogs into closer partnership.

THE SIMILARITIES BETWEEN SCENT WORK AND SPIRITUAL DISCERNMENT

The development of Beau's gift through Scent Work paints a simple, earthy picture of Christian mysticism. Dogs searching for hidden scents mirror the human journey to find God. Just as Beau relied on his natural sense of smell to find what was hidden, followers of Christ are called to develop spiritual senses to recognize God's presence.

In Scent Work, the best handlers do not drag their dogs around the search area; they follow. They learn to trust that the dog's nose is tuned to something real, even when they cannot perceive it themselves. Similarly, the Christian life often involves surrendering our illusion of control and cultivating an open heart to the Holy Spirit's guidance. We still our minds, open our hearts, and let God lead us through subtle cues of grace.

The search area itself can symbolize the spiritual landscape: full of distractions, hidden truths, and unexpected encounters. The handler's role is that of a guide who ultimately follows the dog's lead, reflecting the God–human partnership: God starts the search; we respond with faith and attention. The "alert," when the dog signals a find, is like a moment of revelation, when the searcher suddenly recognizes God's presence amid confusion or pain.

"Scent theory" teaches us that wind, temperature, and humidity influence our sense of smell. Likewise, the climate of our hearts, the faith of our communities, and life circumstances shape our perception of God's presence. The scent of grace can be faint and easily lost if we rush past it. Recognizing it demands sensitivity, patience, and trust, just like Beau's focus on the scent of a scented Q-tip.

Beau's goofy antics in the search area, like his bouncing, his exuberant spirit, and his "caffeine-fueled squirrel" energy, reminded me that spiritual pursuits aren't only about achievement but about joy and relationship. It's easy to turn both faith and dog sports into ladders of accomplishment. Beau nudged me back toward play. He taught me that God often delights in our imperfect enthusiasm and that wonder is found not only at the highest "levels," but in the simple act of showing up together to search.

Trust, surrender, and joy are linked together throughout this story: trust in Beau's nose and in God's guidance; surrender of my need to control every step; joy in every moment of discovery. As Hebrews 11:1 says, "Now faith is confidence in what we hope for and assurance about what we do not see." Beau couldn't see the hidden scent, but he knew it was there. I couldn't tell where God was leading us in our shared journey, but I'm learning to trust that guidance anyway.

Beau's story becomes, for me, a *God-wink* in motion. It is a parable about seeking and being led, about paying attention to what is invisible yet real. His nose, estimated to be tens of thousands of times more sensitive than mine, becomes a living metaphor for the way we are invited to attune our spiritual senses to God's activity in the world. The point is to remain open to wonder and to keep searching with a playful sniff, a wagging tail, and a heart ready for the fragrant mystery of God's presence.

In Beau's story, both of us were changed: he grew from an unwanted, misread dog into a confident partner by my side, and I changed from someone who ignored him on the porch to someone who now more clearly recognizes the gifts God hides in unlikely creatures. Even though his life with me has ended, the wonder of the GHAB that we shared continues to influence how I see God's presence, which is more unexpected than I initially imagined.

My journal entry from 2024 reads:

> *"I love you, Beau. You've reached the end of yourself, and I've reached the end of myself. I will walk with you as far as this earthly road takes us together. Then the Spirit will walk with you the rest of the way, and you will be in better hands than if you stayed with me. As if I had any control over your spirit or mine, I still say, 'I release you, my Beau, Beau,' because I love you. Wait for me. I'll see you again."*

QUESTIONS FOR REFLECTION AND PRACTICE

» Thinking back on the images in this chapter, which scene best inspires hope about what God is doing in the GHAB? How might that story change the "old script" you have about animals or creation?

» This week, pick *one* action that tells a different story: how you paused before dismissing an animal as a nuisance; how you changed how you care for a pet or local wildlife; or how you simply sat with an animal while you prayed. Then, ask yourself: in what way did this act feel like a mustard seed of the Kingdom, and how does it reflect the GHAB?

NOTES

1. "*God-wink*" is adapted from Chris Palmer's discussion in *Winks from Scripture: Understanding God's Subtle Work Among Us* (New Kensington, PA: Whitaker House, 2022).

APPENDIX A

This section is a confession of ecological irresponsibility, shaped by a small Franciscan turn toward creation. When it comes to creation, I often find myself more drawn to St. Francis of Assisi, whose language of "brother sun" reflects a kinship I feel like I'm only beginning to live into.

What follows arises from a different kind of touch, more subtle, perhaps, but no less insistent. In recent years, I have been unsettled by climate change research and reports from the Nature Conservancy (of which I'm a member), as well as by biblical scholars who read Scripture through the lens of the ecological crisis. As I have listened to the mounting evidence of collapsing habitats and diminishing species, I have begun to see how easily I have treated these realities as background noise rather than as a call to repentance. I think of the many times I could have recycled but did not, the plastic I used once and threw away, the convenient bags and bottles I allowed to disappear from my sight without considering where they would go or whom they might harm. None of these acts felt dramatic at the time; they form a pattern of carelessness that my conscience can no longer ignore.

Biblical scholar Ken Stone, whose work explores Scripture, animals, and ecological crisis, reads Psalm 104 as a great song of praise to God for creating and sustaining a beautiful, intricate, interdependent world filled with God's creatures.[1] Humans are included in that praise, but the psalm especially highlights other-than-human animals as those for whom the earth is made and sustained. Those of us who have assumed, often without thinking, that the world exists primarily for our use are mistaken.

According to Stone's reading, "we are given no special consideration apart from the acknowledgment that our sin threatens to unravel God's work."[2] Standing before that psalm and before the witness of the wider creation, I find that my ecological habits are not merely unfortunate; they are in need of confession. This realization is one reason my conscience now insists on speaking.

When read against the background of these contemporary concerns, Psalm 104 is remarkable. It reminds us that some places are for the animals rather than for us, and that there are times for animals and times for humans, distinctions that God has established. To return to the psalm through Elizabeth Johnson's eyes, it "contains no trace of a mandate for human dominion. It is a theocentric depiction of the world that stands as a counterweight to mastery carried out on the assumption that humans have a right to rule other species."[3] We are one species within creation, dependent on your hand for sustenance and life.

A PRAYER OF ECOLOGICAL CONFESSION

Forgive me, Lord, for our part in critically endangering so many species, like sawfish, rays, elephants, sunflower sea stars, monarch butterflies, and countless others, including many of the animals named in Psalm 104: birds, grass-eating beasts, mountain goats, hyraxes, lions, even sea creatures like Leviathan, and the other living creatures of field, forest, and sea. Animals depend on their natural habitats to live; they do not exist independently of them, and every part of creation exists in relation to every other.

Forgive me, Lord, for the ways human greed and indifference have contributed to habitat destruction, poaching, and the careless consumption of the earth's resources.

Forgive me, Lord, for the debilitating effects of climate change, which has altered ecosystems and endangered the biodiversity of waterways and lands.

Forgive me, Lord, for harmful greenhouse gas emissions and for failing to protect forests and other habitats that serve as living carbon. Not all animals are for our use, all the time, as we selfishly imagine.

Forgive me, Lord, for polluting our waterways, land, and air with chemicals that are fatal to animals and plant life.

Forgive me, Lord, for our careless crabbing and fishing, for overfishing, for the collapse of marine food chains, for routinely and unintentionally killing dolphins, sea turtles, seabirds, and others, and for accepting the myth of an inexhaustible sea. Our behaviors fall far short of securing the oceans and seas as you intended, Lord.

We are one species within creation, dependent on your hand, O Lord, for sustenance and life.

Forgive me, Lord, for abusing your creation and exploiting it for excessive gain and selfishness.

Help me, in my finite mind and limited understanding, to relearn the importance of valuing creation, even when I'm unaware of the consequences of my actions, so that my life with your created world may more closely reflect your love.

NOTES

1. Ken Stone, "All These Look to You: Reading Psalm 104 with Animals in the Anthropocene Epoch," *Interpretation* 73, no. 3 (2019): 244.
2. Stone, "All These Look," 245.
3. Elizabeth A. Johnson, *Ask the Beasts: Darwin and the God of Love* (London: Bloomsbury, 2014), 12.

APPENDIX B

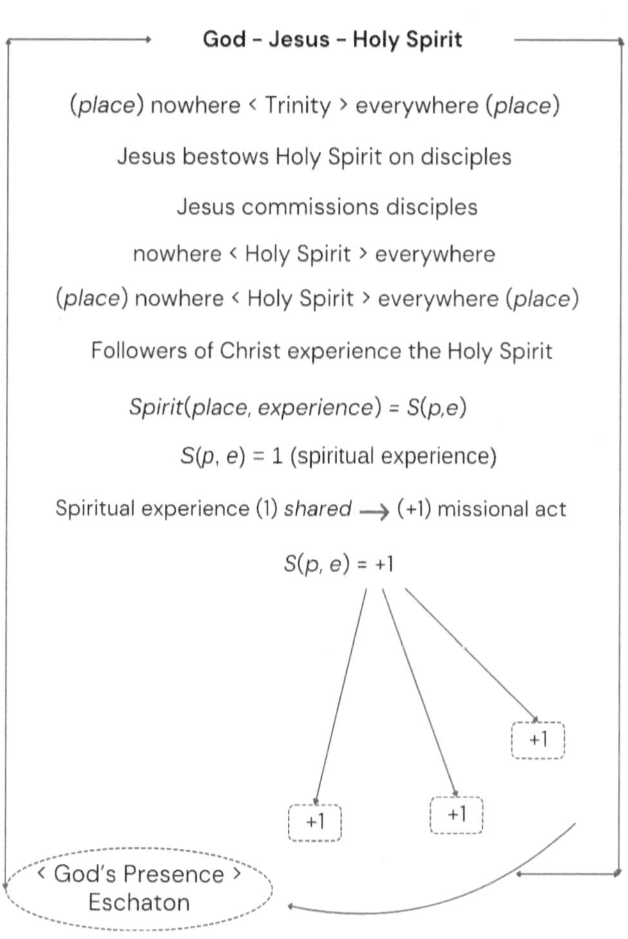

Figure 1. The Missional Unfolding of the Triune God

APPENDIX C

AN IMAGINATIVE RE-TELLING FROM THE ANIMALS' VIEWPOINT

In the beginning, after light was called into being and waters and land were set in their places (Gen. 1:1–10), we sensed the world around us stirring. Seas teemed with life, skies filled with wings, and land pulsed beneath our paws and hooves (Gen. 1:20–25). We did not stand there to witness those first words spoken, yet something in us has always instinctively known that we were called into this world by a Voice. It was as if our bodies, instincts, and migrations all knew to move within an order we did not create.

From the same earth, our Creator then formed a new kind of creature, also from dust, yet set apart for reasons we did not fully understand: the other-than-animals. Humans, we will name them, were made in the Creator's image and entrusted with reflecting our Creator's love and care by "serving and keeping" the garden we shared (Gen. 1:26–28; 2:7, 15). We grazed, flew, swam, and crept under that calling. Some of us were even named by the humans (Gen. 2:19–20); others remained known only to God.

Soon, we saw the garden changed by disobedience (Gen. 3). We watched the serpent's words coil around the hearts of the humans. In their choice, something tore in all of us; the bond between God, humans, and animals frayed, a feeling we could sense in our own bodies. We felt the ground itself groan under thorns and toil, and a sense of fear crept into places once filled with trust. All of us knew that from then on, we would carry the same wound.

Yet even there, we also saw God sew garments for the humans and send them out clothed in a strange mercy (Gen. 3:17–21), a sign that the One who judged had not abandoned any of us, even though that mercy came to them through the grievous, costly gift of our own skins.[1] From that day, our stories and theirs were bound together in a world no longer as it should be, though our Creator never abandoned us.

Through many generations, we saw something more: the Voice of our Creator became flesh and walked among us (Jn. 1:14). We even heard his infant cries echo in a stable, our own body heat warming the air where his mother laid him in a manger (Lk. 2:7, 16). We stepped back to give her room, and our feed trough became his first bed, our breath forming a miniature shelter around the baby we somehow sensed was also our Maker.

Later, we heard his voice call himself the "Good Shepherd" who lays down his life for the sheep (Jn. 10:11). To some of us, he came as the "Lion of the tribe of Judah" (Rev. 5:5), strong and regal; to others, he appeared as a most simple, ordinary human whose hands and heart were kind to all. Some of us in the oceans saw him calm the seas; others watched him touch humans whose wounds marked their bodies, hearts, and minds, and heal them.

We saw him ride into Jerusalem not in a chariot of war but on one of our own, a young donkey, an unclean beast of burden carrying the Creator of the universe (Matt. 21:1–5; Ex. 13:13). Some of us were in the garden that night (Matt. 26:36–46; Mk. 14:32–42; Lk. 22:39–46), making nests in the trees, when we heard our Creator cry out in a kind of pain we had never heard. It seemed to rise into the sky, where some of us circled and brooded. Others of us stood in the shadows of the garden when soldiers led him away to a tree cut into an unusual shape, a shape we, sadly, had seen before. All of us felt the earth tremble when he died (Matt. 27:45, 51). To us, his death was not a theory; it was a shudder through the soil that holds every creature's bones.

Then, one morning, we passed by and saw an empty tomb in another garden (Jn. 19:41–42; 20:1–16). The air was heavy with spices and questions. A woman wept, thinking the body had been taken, until a familiar voice spoke her name (Jn. 20:16). She initially thought he was a gardener, and, in a way, he was, the Creator of all the earth's gardens and, now, of a new creation.

After he returned to the Father, we sensed the wind shift again. In an upper room in the city, there was a sound like a rushing, powerful wind, and something like fire appeared, shining on the people (Acts 2:2–4). We have known that wind from the beginning, when the Spirit hovered over the waters (Gen. 1:2). Now that same Spirit was poured out on humans, both old and young, servants and free (Acts 2:17–18), drawing them into the Creator's life and sending them back into the world as witnesses to all they had seen in the one they called Jesus (Acts 1:8).

Humans might not always realize it, but throughout everything, we animals have also been connected to that Spirit. We feel the Spirit in the springs that water our ravines and give us drink (Ps. 104:10–13), in the nests we build, and in the migrations we cannot completely explain. We understand the truth in what Job's friend said:

> *"But ask the animals, and they will teach you, or the birds in the sky, and they will tell you; speak to the earth, and it will teach you, or let the fish in the sea inform you. Which of all these does not know that the hand of the Lord has done this? In his hand is the life of every creature and the breath of all mankind."* (Job 12:7–10)

We are not sacred Scriptures or sacraments, but again and again, we serve as parables of God's nearness: a raven with bread in its beak (1 Kgs. 17:4–6), our largest neighbor, the fish, holding a prophet in its belly (Jon. 1:17), a donkey seeing an angel when a man does not (Num. 22:21–33), lambs and calves led by a child and lions tamed (Isa. 11:6–9).

From our perspective, what you call the Trinity seems to be an endless cycle of love, giving, and receiving. We sense the invisible pull; it feels like a cosmic embrace reaching into our forests and fields. The Creator, the Fire, and Jesus (cf. Jn. 17:20–23) draw all of us into that love: humans, dogs, donkeys, sparrows, salmon, oaks, and oceans.

The stories you share about us, such as dogs at your feet in grief, horses steadying your fear, birds on the edges of your porches, are, to us, like seeds falling into the soil of a restless world (Mk. 4:3–9). When you respond with love, those seeds begin to grow into a fruit of a Kingdom we also witness, and we hope that one day, that love is endless.

Near the end of your Scriptures, one of your own, John, saw something we have always longed for someone to see. He heard "every creature in heaven and on earth and under the earth and in the sea, and all that is in them" singing together to the One on the throne and to the Lamb (Rev. 5:13). He saw four living creatures, like a lion, an ox, a human, and an eagle, crying "Holy, holy, holy" without ceasing (Rev. 4:7–8). No matter how you interpret these images, we see ourselves there: not as decorations on the edge of salvation, but as voices in the chorus.

Another of your writers, Paul, said that "the creation waits in eager longing for the revealing of the children of God," and that we have been subjected to frustration and "will be set free from [our] bondage to decay and obtain the freedom of the glory of the children of God" (Rom. 8:19–21). We understand that longing. We taste it in polluted streams, as we move through burned forests, in empty nests and overcrowded cages. We also feel it when we are noticed, blessed, and defended; when you tend the land kindly because you recognize it as our home; when you speak to the Creator and allow us to share the space with you; when you let our lives matter in the words you speak and the decisions you make.

Our groaning and your groaning are united in Christ, "through whom" and "for whom" all things were created, and in whom "all things hold together" (Col. 1:16–17). We have seen you wound one another and us; we have also seen you protect, heal, and weep over us.

The joyful and tough times we experience are *not* the whole Kingdom as we often see it. God sometimes lets us start noticing *thin places*, which are the beginning parts of a bigger story unfolding beyond what we currently see. In those moments, our present life with God, humans, and other creatures points beyond itself toward a future we can only partly imagine.

One day, we trust that the One who formed us from the earth and called us good (Gen. 1:25, 31) will make all things new (Acts 3:21; Rev. 21:5). The bonds that now flicker between God, humans, and other creatures will be gathered, purified, and fulfilled in a world where no one harms or destroys "on all [God's] holy mountain" (Isa. 11:9; 65:25).

Until then, every time you notice us, whether refilling a birdbath in summer heat, slowing your car for a deer at dusk, sitting a little longer with an old dog so she does not die alone, freeing a heron from a tangled fishing line, or even leaving a corner of your yard wild for bees and butterflies, you are healing our wounds and easing our suffering. Each choice you make can be an opportunity to see our presence as a gift rather than an interruption, and to offer it as a blessing. In those moments, you live as though the shared Kingdom is already near because in Christ it is, for us as well as for you.

NOTES

1. For representative discussion and one way to interpret this text, see Terence E. Fretheim, *God and World in the Old Testament: A Relational Theology of Creation* (Nashville: Abingdon, 2005), 73–79, who highlights God's ongoing relational care and provision in Gen. 3.

DEFINITIONS

Animal-assisted interventions (AAI) are goal-driven, structured programs that intentionally incorporate animals into health, education, and human services to promote healing and enhance health and wellness. Animal-assisted therapy (AAT), animal-assisted education (AAE), and animal-assisted activities (AAA) are all types of animal-assisted interventions. In all these cases, the animal may be part of a volunteer therapy-animal team supervised by a professional. *(For more information, see https://petpartners.org/publications/glossary/.)*

The terms AAI, AAT, AAE, and AAA are Pet Partners' preferred organizational terms. The phrase "pet therapy" is avoided in the book because it is inaccurate and misleading. It was commonly used decades ago to describe animal-training programs. Currently, the *preferred terms* indicate that the animal serves as *a motivator to enhance the treatment* delivered by a well-trained professional.

Apophatic spirituality (from the Greek apophasis, "negation") describes a way of knowing and loving God that focuses on what cannot be fully expressed or seen about God. It honors God's mystery, hiddenness, and silence. Apophatic practices often involve stillness, unknowing, and trust beyond words, acknowledging that God ultimately surpasses all our images, concepts, and descriptions.

Creation refers to everything God has made in the heavens and on earth, visible and invisible (Gen. 1:1; Isa. 42:5; Ps. 96:11–12; Rom. 1:20). It includes humans, animals, plants, land, seas, stars, and all ecosystems. In this book, "creation" is preferred over "nature," because it emphasizes that the world is not random or self-originating but is beloved and sustained by the Creator.

Kataphatic spirituality (from the Greek kataphasis, "affirmation") refers to a way of knowing and loving God through what can be seen, named, and described: stories, images, creation, sacraments, and relationships. Kataphatic practices use words, symbols, and concrete experiences, such as Scripture, liturgy, and encounters with animals and nature, to help us recognize God's presence and character.

The missio Dei is Latin for "the mission of God." It refers to God's ongoing work of reconciliation, healing, and renewal of all creation. The phrase is rooted in Jesus' words: "As the Father has sent me, I am sending you" (Jn. 20:21). As disciples of Christ, we are invited to participate in this mission by sharing the love, forgiveness, and hope of God's coming Kingdom, both in word and in deed. The concept of *missio Dei* is woven throughout Scripture wherever God sends his people to bear witness to his good news.

Nature/Creation. In this book, I sometimes use the term "*nature*," but I generally prefer "*creation*" because it more clearly points to God as the Creator. When I refer to *nature* or *creation*, I mean the world God has made and sustains, including all living things and the ordered patterns we see in the universe.

Perichoresis is a classical term that describes the mutual indwelling and dynamic relationship among the Father, Son, and Holy Spirit. Early theologians, such as Gregory of Nazianzus, used the image of a dance to express the mystery of the Triune life. John Franke explains that perichoresis shows how the three persons are one by virtue of their interdependent relationality: "The statement 'God is love' refers primarily to the eternal, relational intratrinitarian fellowship among Father, Son, and Holy Spirit." The dance metaphor suggests moving around, making room, and relating to one another without losing identity. It also points to God's loving movement toward creation because the Triune God makes room for creatures without ceasing to be God.

Reception history asks how a biblical text has been *received, imagined, and used* over time in the church's worship, art, preaching, and practice. Rather than focusing only on the text's original setting, reception history traces how generations of believers have pictured, performed, and applied that text in their own contexts.

In this book, I am especially interested in an *animal reception history*: how animals have been present or imagined in these texts and traditions, and how those portrayals, such as animals at the manger, temple sacrifices, or Jesus "with the wild animals" (Mk. 1:13) and how they shape our understanding of the God–Human–Animal Bond (the GHAB).

Revelation means the act of revealing divine truth, even when it is not yet shared with others. More specifically, in Scripture, revelation refers to God's act of revealing or clarifying what was previously wholly hidden or only vaguely perceived (Heb. 1:1).

The **Holy Spirit (Spirit of God or Spirit)** is a person within the Trinity, fully God and personally present. The Spirit sanctifies, heals, and empowers followers of Christ, indicating God's presence in this age and the next. The Holy Spirit is metaphorically like the Holy Link that connects the living world.

Koinonia is a term often translated as fellowship, communion, or participation. It describes the shared life of the church as the body of Christ, grounded not just in social experience but in faith. God, in His very nature, is relational; koinonia extends beyond human fellowship to include our relationships with animals and the wider creation. Koinonia denotes a community of mutual care that encompasses both humans and the animal world.

Human–Animal Bond (HAB) is a term first popularized in the late 1970s by Leo Bustad and Michael McCulloch, with earlier roots in the work of Konrad Lorenz and Boris Levinson. It refers to the mutually beneficial relationship between people and animals, shaped by behaviors essential to the well-being of both. In this book, the HAB is affirmed as real but also expanded to include God's presence and purposes.

God–Human–Animal Bond (GHAB) is a neologism used in this book to denote the spiritual interconnection among God, humans, and animals. It emphasizes the sacred relationship shared among all living beings while affirming that God (G) alone has ultimate authority. Humans (H) are also animals (A), yet are named separately here for clarity. The GHAB does not imply a hierarchy of worth among creatures; instead, it highlights that, from a Christian perspective, there is no meaningful human–animal bond (HAB) apart from God's sustaining love. The GHAB is not merely an extension of the HAB, but a theological construct on its own. The GHAB places the "G" at the center, insisting that God's presence and love undergird every genuine bond between humans and animals, even when we do not recognize God as its source.

BIBLIOGRAPHY

BOOKS

Beale, G. K. *The Temple and the Church's Mission: A Biblical Theology of the Dwelling Place of God*. New Studies in Biblical Theology 17. Downers Grove: InterVarsity Press, 2004.

Brueggemann, Walter. *Genesis*. Interpretation: A Bible Commentary for Teaching and Preaching. Atlanta: John Knox Press, 1982.

Davis, Ellen F. *Scripture, Culture, and Agriculture: An Agrarian Reading of the Bible*. Cambridge: Cambridge University Press, 2009.

Hicks, John Mark, Bobby Valentine, and Mark Wilson. *A Gathered People: Revisioning the Assembly as Transforming Encounter*. Abilene: Leafwood Publishers, 2007.

Hicks, John Mark, Bobby Valentine, and Mark Wilson. *Embracing Creation: God's Forgotten Mission*. Kindle ed. Abilene: Leafwood Publishers, 2016.

Horowitz, Alexandra. *Inside of a Dog: What Dogs See, Smell, and Know*. New York: Scribner, 2010.

Johnson, Elizabeth A. *Ask the Beasts: Darwin and the God of Love*. London: Bloomsbury, 2014.

Knowles, Elizabeth, ed. *The Oxford Dictionary of Quotations*. 8th ed. Oxford: Oxford University Press, 2014.

McKinzie, Greg. *Hermeneutics of Participation*. Eugene: Cascade Books, 2021.

Moltmann, Jürgen. *The Spirit of Life: A Universal Affirmation*. Translated by Margaret Kohl. Minneapolis: Fortress Press, 1992.

Nouwen, Henri J. M. *The Wounded Healer: Ministry in Contemporary Society*. New York: Image Books, 1979.

Palmer, Chris. *Winks from Scripture: Understanding God's Subtle Work Among Us*. New Kensington, PA: Whitaker House, 2022.

Rahner, Karl. "Christianity of the Future." In *Theological Investigations*, vol. 7, *Further Theology of the Spiritual Life*, 149–60. Translated by David Bourke. London: Darton, Longman & Todd; Baltimore: Helicon Press, 1971.

Rahner, Karl. *Concern for the Church: Theological Investigations XX*. Translated by David Bourke. New York: Crossroad, 1981.

Rohr, Richard. *The Universal Christ: How a Forgotten Reality Can Change Everything We See, Hope For, and Believe*. New York: Convergent Publishing, 2019.

Sedmak, Clemens. *Doing Local Theology*. Maryknoll, New York: Orbis Books, 2003.

Way, Kenneth C. *Donkeys in the Biblical World: Ceremony and Symbol*. Winona Lake: Eisenbrauns, 2011.

Wenham, Gordon J. *Genesis 1–15*. Word Biblical Commentary 1. Waco: Word Books, 1987.

ARTICLES AND ONLINE SOURCES

Beck, Alan M. "The Biology of the Human–Animal Bond." *Animal Frontiers* 4, no. 3 (2014): 32–36. *https://www.researchgate.net/profile/Alan-Beck-2/publication/270808642_The_biology_of_the_human-animal_bond/links/55f1bc9008aef559dc492d42/The-biology-of-the-human-animal-bond.pdf.*

Center for the Human–Animal Bond. "About the Continuum." College of Veterinary Medicine, Purdue University. Accessed October 27, 2023. *https://www.vet.purdue.edu/chab/about/continuum.php*.

Darr, Ryan. "The Great Web of Being: Environmental Ethics without Value Hierarchy." *Religions* 15, no. 5 (2024): 520. *https://doi.org/10.3390/rel15050520.*

Dallas Willard Center. "About Dallas." Accessed January 6, 2026. *https://dwillard.org/about-dallas.*

Francis, Pope. "Pope to Vatican Communicators: Build Bridges Where Others Build Walls." *Vatican News.* Accessed May 28, 2025. *https://www.vaticannews.va/en/pope/news/2024-10/pope-to-vatican-communicators-build-bridges-others-build-walls.html.*

Gefter, Amanda. "Finding Peter Putnam." *Nautilus.* Accessed October 27, 2023. *https://nautil.us/finding-peter-putnam-1218035/.*

Hines, Linda M. "Historical Perspectives on the Human–Animal Bond." *American Behavioral Scientist* 47, no. 1 (2003): 7–15. *https://doi.org/10.1177/0002764203255206.*

Horard-Herbin, Marie-Pierre, Anne Tresset, and Jean-Denis Vigne. "Domestication and Uses of the Dog in Western Europe from the Paleolithic to the Iron Age." *Animal Frontiers* 4, no. 3 (2014): 23–31.

Kiprop, Victor. "How Many Animals Are There in the World?" *World Atlas.* March 20, 2018. Accessed April 8, 2022. *https://www.worldatlas.com/articles/how-many-animals are-there-in-the-world.html.*

Magee, David A., David E. MacHugh, and Ceiridwen J. Edwards. "Interrogation of Modern and Ancient Genomes Reveals the Complex Domestic History of Cattle." *Animal Frontiers* 4, no. 3 (2014): 7–22.

Murawski, Roman. "Mathematics and Theology in the Thought of Nicholas of Cusa." *Logica Universalis* 13 (2019): 477–485. *https://doi.org/10.1007/s11787-019-00232-2.*

van Opta, George P. "Exodus 13:13a – The Donkey and the Lamb." *Christian Library.* Accessed May 7, 2022. *https://www.christianstudylibrary.org/article/exodus-1313a-donkey and-lamb.*

Pet Partners. *Pet Partners Therapy Animal Program: Policies and Procedures*. Bellevue, WA: Pet Partners, 2017. Accessed January 26, 2026. *https://petpartners.org/wp-content/uploads/2023/06/PoliciesProceduresTAP_2017-rebranded.pdf.*

Steele, John. "Hope Catches a Tailwind." *Nautilus*, June 6, 2025. *https://nautil.us/hope-catches-a-tailwind-1215966/.*

White Jr., Lynn. "The Historical Roots of Our Ecologic Crisis." *Science* 155, no. 3767 (1967): 1203–7. Accessed December 29, 2025. *https://www.uvm.edu/~gflomenh/courses/ENV-NGO-PA395/articles/Lynn-White.pdf.*

Zinn, Steven A., and Alan M. Beck. "From the Editors: The Human–Animal Bond and Domestication: Through the Ages: Animals in Our Lives." *Animal Frontiers* 4, no. 3 (July 2014): 5–6. *https://doi.org/10.2527/af.2014-0016.*

FURTHER READING AND INFLUENTIAL WORKS IN WRITING THIS BOOK

Augustine. *The City of God.* Translated by Henry Bettenson. New York: Penguin Books, 2003.

Augustine. *The Confessions.* Translated by Maria Boulding. Hyde Park: New City Press, 1991.

Bonaventure. "Breviloquium 2, 5.1, 2." In *Collected Works of St. Bonaventure*, edited by Dominic V. Monti, 72–73. St. Bonaventure, NY: The Franciscan Institute, 2005. Quoted in Richard Rohr, *The Universal Christ: How a Forgotten Reality Can Change Everything We See, Hope For, and Believe.* New York: Convergent Publishing, 2019.

de Chardin, Teilhard. *The Phenomenon of Man.* Translated by Bernard Wall. London: Collins, 1959.

Franke, John R. *Missional Theology: An Introduction.* Grand Rapids: Baker Academic, 2020.

Fretheim, Terence E. *God and World in the Old Testament:*

A Relational Theology of Creation. Nashville: Abingdon, 2005.

Gilmour, Michael. *Eden's Other Residents: The Bible and Animals*. Waco, TX: Baylor University Press, 2014.

Goheen, Michael W. *The Church and Its Vocation*. Grand Rapids: Eerdmans, 2014.

Hjalmarson, Len. *No Home Like Place: A Christian Theology of Place*. Portland: Urban Loft Publishers, 2003.

Hobgood-Oster, Laura. *Holy Dogs and Asses: Animals in the Christian Tradition*. Urbana: University of Illinois Press, 2008.

Holmes, Barbara A. *Joy Unspeakable*. 2nd ed. Minneapolis: Fortress Press, 2017.

Howard, Evan B. *The Brazos Introduction to Christian Spirituality*. Ada: Brazos Press, 2008.

John of the Cross. *Dark Night of the Soul*. Translated by Kieran Kavanaugh and Otilio Rodriguez. New York: HarperOne, 2000.

Julian of Norwich. *Showings*. Translated by Edmund Colledge and James Walsh. Classics of Western Spirituality. New York: Paulist Press, 1978.

Julian of Norwich. *Revelations of Divine Love*. Translated by Elizabeth Spearing. London: Penguin Books, 1998.

Mays, James L. *Psalms*. Interpretation: A Bible Commentary for Teaching and Preaching. Louisville: Westminster John Knox Press, 2011.

McFague, Sallie. *The Body of God: An Ecological Theology*. Minneapolis: Fortress Press, 1993.

Pinnock, Clark H. *Flame of Love: A Theology of the Holy Spirit*. Downers Grove: InterVarsity Press, 1996.

Rohr, Richard. *Dancing Standing Still: A Contemplative Approach to Life*. Cincinnati: St. Anthony Messenger Press, 2005.

Rohr, Richard, Mike Morrell, and William Paul Young. *The Divine Dance: The Trinity and Your Transformation*.

Kindle ed. New Kensington, PA: Whitaker House, 2016.

Rohr, Richard, and Patrick Boland. *Every Thing Is Sacred: 40 Practices and Reflections on the Universal Christ.* New York: Convergent Publishing, 2021.

Sarisky, Darren. *Reading the Bible Theologically.* Kindle ed. New York: Cambridge University Press, 2019.

St. Francis of Assisi. *The Writings of St. Francis of Assisi.* Translated by Peter H. Kwasniewski. New York: New City Press, 2010.

St. John of the Cross. *Dark Night of the Soul.* Translated by E. Allison Peers. New York: Image Books, 1959.

Taylor, John V. *The Go-Between God.* London: Canterbury Press, Norwich, 2004.

Ward, Benedicta, trans. *The Sayings of the Desert Fathers: The Alphabetical Collection.* Kalamazoo: Cistercian Publications, 1984.

White, William R. *Speaking in Stories: Resources for Christian Storytellers.* Minneapolis: Augsburg Publishing House, 1982.

Wintz, Jack, OFM. "St. Francis and the Birds." *Franciscan Media.* Accessed June 1, 2022. *https://www.franciscanmedia.org/franciscan-spirit-blog/st-francis-and-the-birds.*

ABOUT THE AUTHOR

Rev. Dr. Ashley Cooper is an ordained community chaplain with the Federation of Christian Ministry. She holds a Doctor of Ministry from Lipscomb University's Hazelip School of Theology, where her thesis focused on the God–Human–Animal Bond, the central theme of this book.

www.ingramcontent.com/pod-product-compliance
Lightning Source LLC
LaVergne TN
LVHW090513110826
845146LV00003B/836

* 9 7 9 8 9 8 9 9 1 5 4 7 7 *